CIVIL WAR AND
RECONSTRUCTION

DANTES/DSST* Study Guide

© 2018 Breely Crush Publishing, LLC

*CLEP is a registered trademark of the College Entrance Examination Board which does not endorse this book

971091417143

Published by Breely Crush Publishing, LLC
10808 River Front Parkway
South Jordan, UT 84095
www.breelycrushpublishing.com

ISBN-10: 1-61433-043-3
ISBN-13: 978-1-61433-043-1

Printed and bound in the United States of America.

*CLEP is a registered trademark of the College Entrance Examination Board which does not endorse this book.

Table of Contents

United States Society in the Mid-Nineteenth Century

CAUSES OF THE WAR

The Civil War was caused by a separatist conflict when the eleven Southern slave states declared their secession and intent for the expansion of slavery. The Confederate States of America was formed to back the prospect of the expansion, led by President Jefferson Davis (1808-1889), a former statesman who was President of the Confederate States of America.

It was due to the apprehension of the economic depletion that led these states to put together a plan for the growth and expansion of slavery. Those states depended heavily on the slave labor for their crops, especially cotton. Opponents to slavery were concerned about the expansion of slavery, yet both sides knew that if not for the expansion of slavery it would one day slow down or be eliminated altogether.

The United States Federal Government, the Union, led by Abraham Lincoln (1809-1865) opposed secession and rejected any right for the expansion of slavery. Although slavery was illegal in the Northern states, not all were completely against slavery and only a small number of Northerners actively opposed it.

Prior to the election of Abraham Lincoln an arrival of certain structured events helped in the accumulation of the origins of the American Civil War. The election of Abraham Lincoln was one of the main motivations for the formation of the Confederate States of America, in fear that Lincoln would eventually abolish slavery. Each of those events had a multitude of complex political issues, which included federalism, sectionalism, slavery, expansionism, economics, and modernization with each side, the North and the South, taking a very different approach and opinion to each of these concerns.

SOCIAL LIFE IN AMERICA IN THE 1800'S

Preceding the onset of the Civil War and within the first decade of the 19th century, social lifestyles weren't much different than those of the late 18th century. Women continued to wear long flowing skirts, with a blouse typically featuring a long neckline and a separate half-blouse with a high neckline. Shoes were worn not for comfort, but for style and during those years there were not left or right shoes but could fit either foot.

The schools of this era were governed and financially supplied by the local community with very little statewide supervision. Normally the mothers in the community would choose the teacher, usually a man with very little college education himself. Michigan became the first state to enter a statement that promoted the responsibility of the supervision of the public schools.

INDUSTRIALIZATION

Because of trading embargoes, Congress had little power to tax imports from foreign lands until a Congressional meeting in 1787 gave congress the power to tax imports, regulate international trading, and national trading.

The power Congress had to tax and regulate imports into the country pushed them to offending exporting countries. Threats made by the British and the French countries led to the 1807 Embargo, prohibiting American trade with foreign countries. Although the embargo failed, it did force Americans to begin manufacturing their own goods. The end result was industrialization.

Manual power gave way to factories using machinery first driven by waterpower and eventually by steam power. This aided in the massive amount of small farming towns to grow into industrial cities. Large cities began to grow at an alarming rate, such as New York, Boston, Philadelphia and Baltimore. Canals and railroads that were built, making it easier for trading and access to products from the West.

IMMIGRATION

Immigration had both adverse and beneficial effects on the United States during the 19th century. The majority of immigrants came through the United States during the 1830's. Many immigrants sought out the opportunities of the new country – Ireland and Germany providing a large percentage of immigrants. This was due in part to the poverty felt in Ireland, the potato famine, as well as the crop failures in Germany. Individuals who migrated to the United States during those years sent travel tickets and money to family and relatives in their native land, encouraging them to take the journey to the States.

In the late 1700's to early 1800's an estimated 250,000 immigrants found new opportunities in the new country. The largest group to arrive in the early 1800's was the Scotch Irish, and in the year 1801-1802 as many as 20,000 Irish and German citizens came to the United States as immigrants.

The largest amount of the nation's population in the 1800's settled along the eastern seaboard and had increased nearly thirty percent according to the 1790 census. European immigrants mainly worked in factories, built the railroads of the North, and eventually settled their families in the West.

Immigrants coming into to the United States in the early 1830's were near 600,000 strong, four times the amount that came through the century before. The 1860's saw the biggest hike in the population in the history of the United States, 1,427,337 immigrants mostly settling in Minnesota and Wisconsin.

The constant streams of newcomers led to an opposition to immigration. Americans opposing the onslaught of so many newcomers formed structured organizations and secret societies such as the Order of the United Americans and the Know Nothing Party in protest of the surge.

RELIGIOSITY

Religiosity refers to the aspects of religious activity, dedication and belief. Religion was a major part of all social, educational and business matters throughout the 1800's. Just before the mark of the 19th century the US adopted into its constitution the eradication of church and state ties. The First Amendment reads, "Congress shall make no law respecting an establishment of religion, or prohibiting the free exercise thereof."

The majority of the population of Americans practiced the Protestant religion within the beginning of the nineteenth century; there were only a few scattered Catholics and Jews. It was uncommon during the turn of the century to hear of non-Christian religions such as Islam and Buddhist.

More then one million immigrants came to the US between the years of 1845-1855 from Ireland. The majority of these Irish immigrants were Roman-Catholic; these were the first seen Roman-Catholics to immigrate to the United States. The diversity of Religion continued to increase when predominately Lutheran immigrants from Germany came to the US for salvation from the German uprising of 1848.

Many religious groups came to America to elude persecution or the wickedness of their fellow citizens from their country. The lands and openness of the New Country gave immigrants the ability to establish American denominational churches such as the Church of Jesus Christ of Latter-day Saints, Jehovah's Witness, Christian Science Churches, and the Seventh-day Adventist church. These groups relatively came together with the same religious factors, but outside issues such as slavery and other social, educational and political factors resulted in sectional division.

STANDARD OF LIVING

The Northeast felt an economical decrease in agricultural activity caused mainly from the migration of farmers who settled in the West. New England states such as New York, New Jersey and eastern Pennsylvania felt the effects of this decrease the most.

In addition, the shipping and foreign trade industries both were nearly ruined by the economic warfare from the war of 1812.

The 19th century for Western Americans was overwhelmingly rural in its theme, and work was very tough on settlers; they had to clear the lands that were overgrown with forests and debris to form communities and local governments. Life on the frontier was also dangerous; when settlers came in to clear the lands they were meet with hostile Indians. Most settlers were valued more for their capability and enthusiasm to work with their hands rather than their ancestry links or their educational background.

The principles, theories on slavery, economy and social life differed greatly in the South from that of the North. The South's living standards were led by social grace and culture. The Southern slave owners were left with more leisure business matters and social importance. The larger plantations many Southerners kept were filled with cotton, which was the main economical crop, although you could easily find rice fields scattered throughout the South. The larger plantation landowners normally possessed nearly twenty to fifty slaves.

The standard of living however for the slaves was much more disgraceful and discouraging, slaves were often kept in cramped quarters with little, if any, food, daily necessities, medicine, or clothing.

DEMOGRAPHICS

The American Confederation grew from thirteen to thirty six States, which allowed the US to increase in territory, population, and wealth. The frontier territories became heavily populated in the last decade of the 18th, mainly with New Englanders. These frontier territories included Vermont, which became a state in 1791, Kentucky (1792), Tennessee (1796) and Ohio (1803).

The West was characterized by business prosperity until restrictions of business caused economic troubles to the East. Jefferson's Prohibition Trade Act and the War of 1812 were the main causes for those business and economic woes. A second wave of immigrants to place in 1806 resulted in the additions to the Union including Louisiana (1812), Indiana (1816), Mississippi (1817), Illinois (1818), and Alabama (1819).

Just prior to the Gold Rush slightly less than 19,000 individuals found their home near the Pacific Ocean; between the years of 1849 and 1860 more than 280,000 moved west and migrated near the Pacific Ocean.

Growing Differences Between the North and South

The development of differences between the North and the South continued to grow, consisting of issues with slavery, taxes and the territories in the forum of the Congress of the United States. As long as neither side controlled the Senate, compromises were possible. Yet, tensions grew with both parties hoping to acquire new territories after the Louisiana Purchase and the Mexican War. Although the purchase of Alabama in 1819 provided a perfectly balanced Senate, the new territories were soon petitioned by both the North and South for the opportunity to acquire them.

Tensions mounted with the acquisition of the Kansas territory, John Brown's raid, the Dred Scott decision, and the split of the Democratic Party creating larger frustrations between the North and the South. The 1860 election seemed to be the final trigger for secession, and although many attempts for compromise were initiated, they ultimately failed. This set the stage for the Civil War.

SLAVERY AS A SOUTHERN INSTITUTION

The underlining concept of slavery was simple; slaves were considered property. The use of violence and cruelty forced slaves to never forget this particular concept. Although the image of slavery in the South was large plantations with hundreds of slaves and all citizens in the South kept slaves, the truth was only half of Southerners owned slaves and of those, eighty-eight percent owned twenty or fewer. The position of being a slave owner was thought to be only for the privileged and the rich.

Slaves were not only left to the planting and harvesting of the crops, slaves were also made to clear new land, dig ditches, care for and slaughter livestock, make repairs to buildings, and all other labor that came with running a farm or plantation. The grueling labor was always left to the male slaves, while the woman slaves tended to the house work of the plantation: cooking, cleaning, sewing and caring for the children. These slaves were often referred to as house servants, and while house servants benefited from work that was less strenuous then the field servants, they were under constant supervision of their owners.

Many South slave owners found that keeping a slave family together, the mother, father and children, gave them far greater advantages in respect to the economical outcome of crops, yet the majority of slave families were separated and sold off at the auction block.

The cotton gin was one of the most important inventions of the time. It was invented by Eli Whitney in 1793 and was used to separate the cotton from the seeds and seedpods. After this was invented the gin increased the financial benefit and importance of slavery greatly. From 1770-1800 the value of a slave had dropped by nearly fifty percent and the importance of having a slave began to dwindle. A slave on the auction block after the invention of the cotton gin went from $50 to between the prices of $500 to $800.

IMPORTANCE OF COTTON

Before the 18th century, clothing was unsuitable and the garments worn were very difficult to keep clean. Cotton was the major product that could produce suitable garments, but it was also an expensive product. Cotton took time to produce. Before cotton industrialization, in the late 1700's; it took more than twelve to fourteen man-days to produce a pound of cotton. When Eli Whitney invented the cotton gin the cost of producing cotton became dramatically lower, which altered the production of cotton in the US, making it an economical exploitation for the South. Cotton industrialization was even more financially beneficial to the growth of the South.

On the Southern plantations a slave could now produce fifty pounds of raw cotton daily, this was huge compared to the previous amount of time it took a slave to only produce one pound. The process not only helped the Southern plantations produce the cotton faster, but also more cost effectively. The price of cotton a yard fell ninety percent; this caused the demand for cotton clothing to soar soon making it America's largest export.

In the early 1800s Britain, a major purchaser of cotton from the South used more than 79 million pounds of raw cotton, of which forty-eight percent came from the South. Just twenty years later imports were closer to 248 million, seventy percent came from the South and in 1860 over 1,000 million pounds were being used by Britain, while ninety-two percent of that cotton was coming from Southern plantations.

LIVING CONDITION OF SLAVES

Life was hard and work was tough for slaves working in America, quarters were small, crude, susceptible to weather, disease and often without basic necessities. Food was barely enough to keep them from starving, let alone maintain a healthy diet for the heavy workload they endured. Bedding and clothing was also very minimal.

Servant slaves fared far better off than the field servants, because they often were dressed to meet and greet guests and were normally given the hand-me-downs from the mistress of the house. They also had constant access to food in the kitchen and in food stores.

Slaves were often left without medication or care when they would get ill and were often still made to work in the hot and humid conditions of the South. Child mortality was extremely high on plantations, about sixty percent of slave children died. It was much higher for the rice plantations; they held a ninety percent child mortality rate. The constant threat of being sold was far worse for many of the slave families then the thought of acquiring an illness.

When slaves were thought to get out of hand owners would punish the slaves with horrific, hostile and brutal ways such as whipping, torturing, mutilation, imprisonment or being sold. Slaves were forbidden to ever strike an owner or any other white, for any reason even if it was in self-defense. And this was only one of the appalling rules laid out by Congress for slaves called the slave codes.

Although every state carried their own sets of codes and every states codes varied, the basic rules included, slaves were considered property and they were to be treated as just that, slaves could not testify in court against a white, they could not make contracts, buy or sell goods, own firearms, possess anti-slavery literature, gather without whites present, or visit the homes of whites or free blacks. The killing of a slave was almost never murder and the rape of a slave woman was treated as a form of trespassing.

🎓 Abolition Movement

The abolition movement began long before the time emancipation came about. The first great awakening began in the late 18th century, and the second in the early 19th century at the time of colonial settlements and mainly consisted of religious revivals and meetings. The meetings promoted the notion that all humans were free to renounce their sins and achieve salvation. They also posited that slavery was a byproduct of personal sin and they implied that emancipation was the price for repentance. This message came to the conclusion that a person should save their neighbors. Southern Kentucky was home to the first of such meetings with more than 10,000 participants.

In 1833 the American Anti-Slavery Society was founded and their (estimated) tens of thousands of members condemned slavery as a racial discriminating practice and as a moral sin. Many of these groups met opposition from slaveholders and rejections from national religious institutions. Opponents attempted to suppress the groups with enactments from churches and states and by using mob violence.

Many followed the lead of William Lloyd Garrison, who abandoned the churches believing they were corrupted by slavery. Garrison wanted to achieve a universal reform including the extension of women's rights, pacifism and temperance. The American Anti-Slavery Society committed to the political practices of Garrison and began to advocate for the dissolution of the Union with slave holding states. Garrison also used radical techniques to awaken Northerners by appointing a woman, Maria Weston Chapman, as the overseer of the society's main office. Garrison also used women for traveling lecturers such as Sojourner Truth, Elizabeth Cady Stanton, Abby Kelley, Lucy Stone and dozens more women who all met with opposition and threats of physical harm.

Religious abolitionists formed the American and Foreign Anti-Slavery Society. This group continued to lobby religious institutions and gained valuable associates in the 1840's from the Methodist, Baptist and Presbyterian churches. Their resolve to gain anti-slavery support from religious institutions often caused the division of many local religious foundations.

These political and religious groups continued to focus their attention on the dismantling of slavery and made major gains until the Civil War, especially during the 1850's. Though they continued to grow in membership through the abolition movement, they still remained a minority and few free blacks in the Northern states received equal treatment.

LEADERS

Some abolition groups supported the abolition movement through churches and other organizations, while others used the political scene. Politically focused abolitionists lobbied legislatures and grilled political candidates on issues of slavery. The federal government's resistance to the lobbying and petitioning of these groups forced political abolitionists to form their own party to pursue emancipation in 1840 called the Liberty Party.

Several of the abolition leaders came from New England including William Allen, the founding member and director of the African Institution who assisted for many years as a committee member of the Society for the Abolition of the Slave Trade. Henry Ward Beecher was another, the brother to Harriett Beecher Stowe who authored the famous book *Uncle Tom's Cabin* and was supporter of emancipation. John Brown was the first white American to advocate and practice insurrection as a means to the abolition of slavery. Wendell Phillips, a graduate from Harvard Law School, stopped practicing law in 1836 to dedicate himself to the abolitionist cause of William Lloyd Garrison. Theodore Dwight Weld was one of the leading founders of the American abolition movement and played a key role as a writer, editor and speaker. He is best known for his work American Slavery as It Is: Testimony of a Thousand Witnesses. Arthur Tappan was the co-founder of the American Anti-Slavery Society and served as its first President until he resigned when the group began to support woman suffrage and feminism. He and his brother then founded the American and Foreign Anti-Slavery Society. Robert Purvis, member of a prominent family in South Carolina, helped establish the

American Anti-Slavery Society and the Library Company of Colored People. He was a large supporter of the Underground Railroad and is estimated to have helped one slave escape to freedom a day. By that account he would have helped 9,000 people find freedom.

These were only a few of the major leaders in the resolution of slavery. Other prominent leaders in the fight for emancipation from the start of the country included; John Quincy Adams, John Jay, Alexander Hamilton, Aaron Burr, Sojourner Truth, Elizabeth Cady Stanton, John Rankin, Henry Stanton, James Sherman, John Parker, and many others.

METHODS AND TACTICS OF ABOLITION

One of the first methods of abolitionists was to spread the word and gather like-minded individuals together. It was when this method began that the formations of many abolition groups were formed. One such group was the American Anti-Slavery Society who focused on putting together lectures in an attempt to show the moral and religious consequences of slavery, hoping to change the minds and hearts of non-slaveholders. Many abolition groups found these tactics to be inadequate and they turned their attention to more political methods.

Another method abolitions used to get their message out was through published literature. This tactic included the publication of pamphlets and leaflets that included sermons, songs, essays, poetry and slogans that included an anti-slavery message. They also attempted to show the cruelty and animalist means of slavery through children's literature, attempting to awaken a younger audience and following, although this sort of literature was outlawed in the Southern states.

Newspapers were also important to abolitionists to get their message across. The Liberator, published by William Lloyd Garrison, was one of many newspapers that attacked the immoral sanction of slavery.

One of the most famous activities and tactics of the abolition movement was the Underground Railroad where slaves were given the means to escape from slavery as well as the shelter, safety and guidance to be free. The Underground Railroad stretched from the Southern states all the way to Canada and was the first method where slaves could find solitude and safety from their slaveholders.

UNCLE TOM'S CABIN

The novel *Uncle Tom's Cabin* by Harriet Beecher Stowe, was about the evils of slavery and was influential in creating sentimental feelings against the institution of slavery. The tale centered on Uncle Tom, a long suffering black slave and the other slaves and owners that revolved around his life. It depicted the cruel realities of slavery as it showed the Christian values that love and faith can overcome anything evil, even slavery.

The novel was the best-selling novel of the 19th century and has been said to be a main source of the abolition movement. 300,000 copies of the book were sold the first year it was published in 1852. Its impact was so strong it was said to have laid the groundwork for the American Civil War – so much so that when the writer met with Abraham Lincoln he was said to have commented, "So, this is the little lady who made this big war."

Westward Expansion of Free and Slave Territory

In the mid-1800's the US attained large new territories in the West; new territories including Texas, the Oregon region, California and New Mexico. It was Andrew Jackson who promised to expand the US West, stating Americans had the right and the duty to extend its civilization. This theory fueled the westward move to Indian and Mexican territories. With the extent of new territories a struggle over whether slavery should be permitted in the new territories erupted between the North and South.

Jackson not only felt the Westerm territories had to be established but also the lands in the Southeast, where he seized millions of lands from the Indian nations. The majority of the land Jackson seized became established cotton plantations, while the five different Indian nations were forced from their homes and made to move west. Although many Indian tribes retaliated with brutal wars, many pursued the journey with a promise of $9,000,000 for their lands. The westward journey was met with a quarter of the Indians dying; the Cherokee Indians named this journey the "Trail of Tears."

After the Alamo, Texas clammed its independence and in 1845 obtained its annexation into America, after the Mexican-American War America also gained the New Mexico and California territories.

MISSOURI COMPROMISE

In 1818 Missouri sought admission to the Union with a constitution to permit slavery. Northerners feared that once Missouri was given admission as a slave state it would serve as a standard for admission of all future States, creating an America that is unbalanced.

Two years of a bitter battle over the admission, the battle seemed to heading for the Civil War until a compromise was made between the Union and the Continental United

States, known as the Missouri Compromise. The compromise admitted Missouri to the Union of a slave state in a compromise to admit Maine as a free state, thus keeping a balance in the senate. A line was drawn for Missouri's Southern boundary and slavery would not be allowed in the territory north of that line excluding the state of Missouri.

Controversy did not end with the Missouri Compromise, it only allowed the attention of slavery to grow for the abolition of slavery. While the Missouri compromise gave Northerners a more focused and comprehensive sentiment regarding the ethical grounds of slavery, and it infuriated Southerners. The North, more stern over the matter, felt slavery needed to be abolished either gradually with compensation for the slave owner or immediately. The South grew impatient with the North and felt the very basic of their economy and social order was being threatened. The South instantly took political action; first, they passed firmer laws that keep their slaves under control. Secondly, they secured passage with Congress for the gag order, provided that Congress would not consider any petition in on the subject of slavery. And lastly, also unsuccessfully, they attempted to shut out mail circulation that included anti-slavery literature.

The diversity between the North and the South before, during and after the Missouri compromise only created more tension between the two and is said to be the major start to the Civil War.

MEXICAN WAR

In the wake of the 1845 annexation of Texas, in which Mexico refused to recognize the secession of Texas in 1836 and announced its intention to take Texas back, a military conflict began between the United States and Mexico. Although the United States viewed the war as a partisan issue, Mexico considered the war as a matter of national pride.

Mexico had much land to lose. After the Mexican War of Independence, which resulted in its becoming the first Mexican empire in 1823, it inherited ownership of the providences of California, New Mexico, Colorado, Utah, Arizona, and Texas. General Santa Anna and the Mexican government attempted to centralize power, yet many of the Mexican states rebelled against this government, including Texas and California.

Texas was disconcerted regarding the abolition of slavery in Mexico and the abolition of the federalist constitution in exchange for a more centralized government under the direction of Santa Anna. Uproar over these grievance issues began in Texas and is known today as the Texas Revolution.

Texas established diplomatic ties with the United Kingdom and the United States, as most Texans were in favor of annexation by the United States. The US was divided on the acceptance of Texas, as Northerners feared that another slave state would give more power to the slave-holding states, making the country out of balance.

When the Mexican government established a border between Mexico and Texas along the Nueces River, Texas moved the border closer to the Rio Grande, which gave Texas more land, the eruption of this dispute lead to the Mexican-American War. Once the Mexicans moved in and attacked General Zachary Taylor and his 1,500 troops that had settled along the Nueces River Congress overwhelmingly approved the declaration for war.

Mexico ultimately lost the war and as a result lost more than 500,000 square miles of land, almost half of its territory, which are today known as New Mexico and California. More than 1,000 Mexican families resided in California and 7,000 in New Mexico once these territories became a part of the US, some families moved back to Mexico but the majority stayed and became American citizens.

COMPROMISE OF 1850

The North continued to be enraged by slavery, as the South defended it with more persistence. After the Mexican War the United States felt a new crisis; antislavery forces demanded that slavery be abolished from any lands surrendered by Mexico, which included New Mexico, Arizona, California, and the present Rocky Mountain states.

Congress was so confused and divided over the anti-slavery and slavery groups that no solution could be reached. In January 1850 Henry Clay introduced into legislation a series of compromises between the North and South. Over the next seven months and various changes into the compromise; it was passed in August and came to be known as the Compromise Measures of 1850.

This compromise admitted California as a free state and set up territorial governments in the remainder of the Mexican cession to decide for themselves whether to permit slavery or not.

KANSAS-NEBRASKA ACT

Illinois Senator Stephen A. Douglas introduced the Kansas-Nebraska Act which revoked the Missouri compromise and provided that settlers in the territories should decide for themselves "all questions pertaining to slavery." Northerners felt that Douglas was only attempting to gain the confidence and win the South's support as the Presidential nominee of the Democratic Party in the 1856 election. Passing the Kansas-Nebraska act incurred hostilities from both the North and the South. Not only did it provoke another arousal of conflict between the North and South, but it also stirred tensions between abolitionist and pro-slavery inclined immigrants who settled in Kansas. The

Kansas-Nebraska Act also held its own destructive measures within political parties. It is attributed with the dismemberment of the Whig Party when it forced a wedge between those Southern members who supported the measure and those who opposed it. The most important long term corollary of the act was the creation of the Republican Party.

BIRTH OF THE REPUBLICAN PARTY

When the Democratic Republican Party (shortened to be the Democratic Party) and the Whig party disagreed about slavery, the Republican Party was formed. The formation of the Republican Party is credited directly to the Kansas-Nebraska act. The founder of the party denounced slavery as sheer evil and opposed it altogether. They demanded the revocation of the Kansas-Nebraska Act and the Fugitive Slave Law. The party maintained that the Northerner's free labor system was superior to the slave labor system, and largely absorbed members of the Free Soil Party, who sought to confine slavery to its existing boundaries.

THE KANSAS WARS

Despite the opposition of the settlers, the violence throughout Kansas was kept to a minimum until the Kansas territory elections in 1855. The election result was overwhelmingly composed in favor of proslavery. Although the end result lay in favor of pro-slavery, not all were in favor of the pro-slavery movement and a multitude of violent episodes and small wars erupted in the Kansas territories from 1855-1858. This time period has come to be known as "Bleeding Kansas."

The wars that erupted throughout Kansas included the Wakarusa War, Sacking of Lawrence, and the Pottawatomie Massacre. A number of Territorial constitutions were implemented to put an end to the division and violence Kansas encountered. Those constitutions included the Topeka Constitution, Lecompton Constitution, Leavenworth Constitution, and the Wyandotte Constitution.

Once the Wyandotte Constitution was in place, Kansas was admitted as a free state, and with the departure of John Brown from the state, the violence virtually ended in 1859.

THE ELECTION OF 1856

The newly formed Republican Party held its first convention in 1856. The Party nominated John C. Fremont of California for President, while the Democrat Party nominated James Buchanan of Pennsylvania. The American Party placed in the third candidate, former President Milliard Fillmore.

Fillmore's campaign stressed the ability to restore order and harmony back to the states. While the Republican Party attempted to focus public attention on the disasters of Kansas, the Democrats succeeded in convincing the public that the Republicans were extremists who were set on destroying the Union. Buchanan carried the election, even though the Republican Party made significant progress during the elections.

DRED SCOTT DECISION

Dred Scott's case holds a unique place in American constitutional history as an example of the Supreme Court trying to impose a judicial solution on a political problem. It called down enormous criticism on the Court and on Chief Justice Roger Brooke Taney - a later chief justice, Charles Evans Hughes, described it as a great "self-inflicted wound."

Scott, born a slave, had been taken by his master, an army surgeon, into the free portion of the Louisiana territory. Upon his master's death, Scott sued for his freedom, on the grounds that since slavery was outlawed in the free territory, he had become a free man there, and "once free always free." The argument was rejected by a Missouri court, but Scott and his white supporters managed to get the case into federal court, where the issue was simply whether a slave had standing - that is, the legal right-- to sue in a federal court. The first question the Supreme Court had to decide was whether it had jurisdiction. If Scott had standing, then the Court had jurisdiction, and the justices could go on to decide the merits of his claim. But if, as a slave, Scott did not have standing, then the Court could dismiss the suit for lack of jurisdiction.

The Court ruled that Scott, as a slave, could not exercise the prerogative of a free citizen to sue in federal court. That should have been the end of the case, but Chief Justice Taney and the other Southern sympathizers on the Court hoped that a definitive ruling would settle the issue of slavery in the territories once and for all. So they went on to rule that the Missouri Compromise of 1820 was unconstitutional since Congress could not forbid citizens from taking their property, i.e., slaves, into any territory owned by the United States. A slave, Taney ruled, was property, nothing more, and could never be a citizen.

The South, of course, welcomed the ruling, but in the North it raised a storm of protest and scorn. It helped create the Republican Party, and disgust at the decision may have played a role in the election of Abraham Lincoln in 1860.

Despite the fact that Buchanan hoped to end the agitation over the slavery issue his administrative only brought the issue to a final crises and the South won victoriously. In 1857 the US Supreme Court declared that slaves were property and had no rights as citizens and that Congress has no right to prohibit slavery in the territories.

Within that same year Kansas managed to have the state adopt the pro-slavery Constitution, yet a majority of the citizens opposed the constitution. Buchanan recommended to the Senate that Kansas be admitted as a state under its provisions; the bill passed in the senate but was defeated by the house. And Kansas was finally admitted into the Union as a free state in 1861. Just before Kansas was admitted as a free state, a number of debates ensued between Abraham Lincoln and the senator of Illinois, Stephen Douglas. These debates brought the attention of the political and moral aspects of slavery throughout the country. Lincoln stood for congressional control over slavery, while Douglas advocated for popular sovereignty. Even though Douglas won the election the incidents placed Abraham Lincoln in the seat of the leader of the Republican Party.

JOHN BROWN'S RAID ON HARPER'S FERRY

In the late hours of October 16, 1859 a raid, which started its journey across the Potomac River from Maryland to Virginia, was in motion. Lead by John Brown the main objective of the raid was to capture US arsenals that were stored on Harper's Ferry. Although initial success was met the group, comprised of sixteen white and five black men, the raiders unknowingly would find themselves trapped in a town they attempted to isolate.

Upon John Brown and his group's arrival they were able to apprehend the arsenal and other armory they sought after, as well as the capture of 60 townspeople. One of the raiders stopped a B&O railroad train in an attempt to detain it, but the train was permitted to take its original journey. Once that train reached its destination Federal troops were sent to rescue the town at Harper's Ferry.

The group found themselves and the entire town surrounded by militant forces. With only nine hostages left, Federal forces stormed into the small firehouse wounding John Brown in the process. John Brown was convicted of treason, his last words before his hanging made this final statement, "I, John Brown, am now quite certain that the crimes of this guilty land will never be purged away but with blood."

Political Situation in 1860

The South became unsatisfied with the specifications of the popular sovereignty and its leaders demanded that congress protect slavery where it existed and where it did not. The North and South began to split into two very different regions; each had economic, social and political differences that created stiff tensions, although compromises were made that kept the Union together for many years.

Despite the Democratic Party's inability to get together and stay together during their three previous conventions and put in place a candidate for the 1860 Presidential elections, the Republican Party found themselves met with opposition that threatened the coming of a Civil War. Yet, the Republicans had an almost unbeatable advantage in the Electoral College, given that they dominated almost every Northern state.

Loyalty to one's state took precedence over loyalty to one's country, and the Union was considered to be a voluntary compact. Northerners depended greatly on a governmental infrastructure for the building of roads and railways. Southerners felt no need for it; they also feared should there be a government it would interfere with slavery.

SPLIT IN DEMOCRATIC PARTY

The Democratic Party was split over issues of slavery and at a Democratic convention in Charleston fifty Southern Democrats walked out over partisan issues. The Democrat Party had six candidates including, Stephen Douglas of Illinois, Andrew Jackson of Tennessee, Daniel Dickinson of New York, Joseph Lane of Oregon, James Guthrie of Kentucky, and Robert Mercer Taliaferro Hunter of Virginia. Douglas was ahead on the first ballot; he only needed fifty-seven more votes, but was fifty votes short of a nomination. Again on May 3rd the Democratic Party adjourned, and then met again on June 18th.

Once again they met and once again Democrats walked out over the divided resolution of slavery in the territories, this time 110 delegates walked out. This split left the remaining Democrats to nominate Stephen Douglas of Illinois as President and Herschel Vespasian Johnson of Georgia for Vice President. Southern Democrats reconvened and on June 28th nominated Joseph Lane of Oregon for President and John Cabell Breckenridge or Kentucky for Vice President. This forced the Democrats to split and create a Northern Democratic Party and a Southern Democratic Party.

REPUBLICAN PARTY

Former Whigs, Free-Soilers, and Northern Democrats who opposed the expansion of slavery came together and established the Republican Party in 1854. It was created as an act of rebellion against the Slave Power, a term used for the slaveholders in the South who aspired to control the federal government and expand slavery across the nation.

John C. Fremont was the first Republican to run for office of the Presidency in 1856 as the Republican candidate, though he lost the Presidential election the Republican Party showed to be a foundation.

In 1860 the newly elected Abraham Lincoln was the first Republican in the Presidential office, many Republican still refers to this era as the party of Lincoln. After the election of Lincoln the party passed into Congress major legislature that promoted rapid modernization, a national banking system, high tariffs, paper money issued with backings, a huge national debt, homestead laws, and land grants to aid higher education, railroads and agriculture.

ABRAHAM LINCOLN

Abraham Lincoln was a major opponent of the expansion of slavery, a political leader in the western states, who was the first Republican Party nomination to win the presidency. While in office he led the defeat of secessionist Confederacy, the American Civil War, and introduced measures that ultimately resulted in the abolition of slavery.

Horace Greeley was the editor of the New York Times and wrote an editorial entitled "The Prayer of Twenty Millions" which called for the immediate emancipation of all slaves. Lincoln wrote a response which was published on the front page on August 25, 1862:

"If I could save the Union without freeing any slave, I would do it; and if I could save it by freeing all the slaves, I would do it; and if I could do it by freeing some and leaving others alone, I would also do that."

In 1863, Lincoln issued his Emancipation Proclamation and promoted the passage of the thirteenth Amendment to the Constitution in 1865.

At the end of the war Lincoln took a liberal view on reconstruction and sought speedy reconciliation policies with the nation. Lincoln was admired for his powerful messages and speeches such as his Gettysburg Address. Yet he was also met with severe criticism on issues such as his refusal to compromise on slavery, for war measures, and many criticized him for not abolishing slavery soon enough and for not being ruthless enough.

Lincoln was considered to be a wise man, and many of his quotations we remember and repeat today:

That this nation, under God, shall have a new birth of freedom, and that government of the people, by the people, for the people, shall not perish from the earth.

Let us have faith that right makes might; and in that faith let us to the end, dare to do our duty as we understand it.

It is not best to swap horses while crossing the river.

Truth is generally the best vindication against slander.

Beware of rashness, but with energy and sleepless vigilance go forward and give us victories.

The Almighty has his own purposes.

Men are not flattered by being shown that there has been a difference of purpose between the Almighty and them.

In giving freedom to the slave we assure freedom to the free - honorable alike in what we give and what we preserve.

Nobody has ever expected me to be president. In my poor, lean lank face nobody has ever seen that any cabbages were sprouting.

I shall try to correct errors when shown to be errors, and I shall adopt new views so fast as they shall appear to be true views.

You can fool some of the people all of the time, and all of the people some of the time, but you can not fool all of the people all of the time.

Why should there not be a patient confidence in the ultimate justice of the people? Is there any better or equal hope in the world?

I pray that our Heavenly Father may assuage the anguish of your bereavement and leave you only the cherished memory of the loved and lost, and the solemn pride that must be yours to have laid so costly a sacrifice upon the altar of freedom.

ELECTION RESULTS

The 1860 election set the final ultimatum for the Civil War, as the political system split four ways. This only proved that the nation in its current state could not hold together the Union. The tensions the nation faced throughout the previous sixty years slowly brought the state of affairs to unstable grounds with issues including state rights and slavery.

These issues led to bringing Abraham Lincoln and the Republican Party into power without one Southern state behind them; in fact Lincoln was not even on the ballots in Southern states.

The election of 1860 was a textbook version on how to win an electoral majority without the popular majority, Lincoln achieved less than forty percent of the popular vote. The division of the nation led him to collect seventeen states plus four electoral votes in New Jersey for a total of 180 electoral votes. Lincoln still would have won even if sixty percent of voters had banned together to vote for one of the other candidates, Democrat Stephen A. Douglas of the Southern Democrats, or John C. Bell of the new Constitutional Union Party. Besides California, Oregon, and Illinois, Lincoln won every state that cast its electoral votes for him. As the result of the election, South Carolina made it secession from the United States, followed by others that soon formed the Confederate States of America.

1861

In 1861, just after the election of President Lincoln, tension within the states led even more states to secession. Both sides attempted to strengthen their manpower with volunteers and to meet the demand of supplies for their armies. The Confederate Army was formed within the early months of 1861 and battles such as Fort Sumter and the First Manassas ensured the beginning of the Civil War.

SECESSION

Secession is the act of withdrawing from an organization, union or political entity, normally caused by a very strong opposing difference. Starting with South Carolina, seven states declared secession from the Union and initially formed the Confederate States of America, a Southern government that took control of federal forts and properties within their boundaries. In order of secession, these states were South Carolina, Mississippi, Florida, Alabama, Georgia, Louisiana, and Texas. Jefferson Davis became the President of the Confederacy. Their government modeled the U.S. Constitution but included provisions that allowed for slavery.

President Buchanan only made this statement, "The South has no right to secede, but I have no power to prevent them."

In the months following the formation of the Confederate States of America, North Carolina, Virginia, Arkansas, North Carolina, and Tennessee all left the Union.

SOUTH CAROLINA'S ROLE

South Carolina was the first state to secede from the United States; it had longed for an excuse to secede to unite the Southern states against the Anti-Slavery forces and declared, "The Union now subsiding between South Carolina and other states under the name of the United States of America is hereby dissolved."

Although the Civil War started over the dispute about slavery, it was continued by disputations about state rights. South Carolina stated that the Northern States were not fulfilling their federal obligations which included:

- The refusal to enforce fugitive slave codes
- They denied the rights of property
- Assisted runaway slaves to leave their homes and find safety
- The election of Lincoln
- Giving citizenship to persons that were incapable of being citizens

South Carolina was the first state to secede from the Union to form the Confederate States of America, followed by Mississippi, Texas, Alabama, Florida, Georgia, and Louisiana. These states sent delegates to Montgomery Alabama and adopted provisions for the newly formed Confederate States of America in 1861.

BORDER STATES

The Border States refer to the five slave states of West Virginia, Missouri, Maryland, Delaware and Kentucky. These five states were on the border between the Northern Union states and the Southern Confederate states. These states were sub-divided between the Union and Confederate governments and had political, social, geographical and economical connections with both the North and South and were critical in the outcome of the Civil War.

GOVERNMENT OF CONFEDERATION

A confederation is an association of sovereign states or communities, usually created by treaty yet often adopting a common constitution. In this instance, the confederation was the Confederate States of America. Jefferson Davis was nominated as the President of the new Confederate States of America for a six-year term.

The Confederate States of America reported their constitution, by which the new government was formed, and the Provisional Congress adopted it on March 11, 1861, the constitution varied from that of the Constitution of the United States of America.

FORT SUMTER

The Battle of Fort Sumter was the first military engagement of the Civil War. It began at Fort Sumter in Charleston Harbor, South Carolina. United States Major Robert Anderson's force was positioned in South Carolina when the state seceded. Confederate patience for Anderson's presence soon wore thin. Fearing for his men, Anderson relocated to Fort Sumter, reporting limited supplies. On Thursday, April 11, 1861, Confederate General Beauregard demanded that Anderson surrender. He refused. At 4:30 A.M. the following morning, the Confederates opened fire. Anderson's troops didn't return fire for two hours. The fort's supply of ammunition was not suited for an equal fight, and Anderson struggled to ration his ammunition. On Saturday, April 13, Anderson surrendered the fort. The battle had lasted a mere thirty-six hours in total. No soldiers died on either side during the battle.

BLOCKADE

Shortly after the beginning of the Civil War, President Lincoln announced a blockade against the trading ports along the Southern coast. He hoped that cutting off their supplies would force the end of the conflict. However, the Naval Force in the North was not sufficient to guard the entire Southern coast, and Britain referred to it as a 'paper blockade.' In other words, because the Union did not have the ability to enforce the blockade it existed only on paper. Their trade continued as the Union sought to quickly build their Naval Force, employing any vessel capable of holding weapons to guard the Southern coasts. The blockade was never entirely executed, but by the end of the war it was sufficient enough to make trade extremely difficult for many Southern cities, and inflation was rampant.

FIRST MANASSAS (BULL RUN)

In Manassas Junction, Southwest of Washington D.C., General Irvin McDowell and the Union army began to move toward Confederate troops on July 16, 1861, President Lincoln appointed McDowell to command the Army of Northeastern Virginia and engage against the Confederate Army. The Confederate Army of the Potomac was settled near Manassas Junction, just outside of the United States capital. McDowell's plan was to swoop down on the army, preventing them from enforcing Beauregard.

Once the two armies meet on July 21, 1861 the battle of the first Bull Run began, also known as the First Manassas. The battle began in the Northerners favor, it was when Confederate forces called for reinforcements and General Thomas Jackson, who earned the nickname "Stonewall" arrived that the tide turned in favor of the Confederacy. The battle ended with victory to the South.

With the conclusion of First Bull Run, Northerners soon visualized the Civil War as a grim struggle that could last for more years then they originally projected. The Union soon called in General George McClellan and pushed for the organization of long-term volunteers. General McClellan took charge of the Union troops around the capital enforcing intense training and discipline. By the end of October his well-trained army came to be known as the Army of the Potomac. They remained inactive under the watchful eye of McClellan who was receiving criticism from the administration and the public alike, which was where the phrase "All quiet on the Potomac" originated.

Union Army vs. Confederate Army

Because the war was fought over such a large area of the South, the Confederacy and the Union had to have several armies that were assigned to different theatres in the country.

The Union Army, also known as the Northern Army or the Federal Army, was only 16,000 strong when the Civil War began in 1861, but by this time men had already began to resign and joining the new Confederate Army. Other names for the Union armies included Union Army, Union Army of the Potomac, Union Navy, Union Blockade, and Union Cavalry. It is a misconception that the South held the advantage over the North, in fact the number of professional officers in the Union totaled 642 as opposed to only 283 for the Confederate. In total it is estimated that two and a half million soldiers fought for the Union army.

The Confederate Congress formed the Confederate army in 1861; also Confederate States Navy and the Confederate States Marine Corps. During the Civil War an estimated 1,500,000 men served for the army and fought for them in the war, although accurate record keeping did not begin until late in the war. The Confederate Army was actually three organizations including the Army of the Confederate States of America, the Provisional Army of the Confederate States and the State Militias. They did not have a military commander until late in the war; this was a major weakness in the Confederacy, some consider it the reason for the ultimate failure and surrender of the army in 1865.

The Confederate Army was composed of independent armies and military departments. Each of those departments were normally named after their respected state or region.

PREPAREDNESS

The North seemed to hold the advantage in the war with a combined population of nearly 22 million people. The North had the majority of the factories that produced war material and they had extensive railroad connections which served as an important transportation unit for maintaining worldwide commerce.

The population of the South was a relatively meager 9 million. Southern commanders, on the other hand, were far more experienced than those of the North. The South also held the defensive position and had only to defend their lands. Although the South was made up of farms and plantations that produced materials wanted by the European world, they had few ships and their ports were closed not long after the war began.

The North and the South each had problems unifying their respective states throughout the duration of the war. The North had copperheads, draft rioters, bounty jumpers, and many Northerners became very tired of the war a long time before it ended. The South commonly had draft dodgers, tax evaders and profiteers who preferred to run luxuries through the blockade as opposed to war supplies.

VOLUNTEERS

Most soldiers on each side of the war were volunteers. Volunteering during the Civil War was motivated by a sense of pride for men who enlisted, although many men joined to ensure a steady paycheck and food during their duty. Both armies depended heavily on volunteers to fight.

As the Civil War broke out each Union state was given a quota of volunteer regiments to be provided for service in the Civil War in the United States Army. Each service would not be less than three months and could last up to three years. Southern states also raised and supplied the Confederate Armies with volunteers. By 1863, many of the regiments, from both armies, were mainly constructed of volunteers who had been in service sense the beginning of the war in 1861.

THEATER OPERATIONS

During the Civil War there were three separate theater operations the Eastern Theater, the Western Theater, and the Trans-Mississippi. A theater is an area where a battle is being fought. Usually, a war must be fought over a large expanse of land in order to have multiple theaters. Theaters use natural boundaries such as rivers to divide areas of engagement (war) into different theaters.

The Eastern Theater included the states of Virginia, West Virginia, Maryland, Pennsylvania, the District of Columbia and the seaports of North Carolina. Some of the most famous campaigns were strategies conspired by the Eastern Theaters. Under Robert E. Lee the Eastern Theater saw the battles of Gettysburg, Antietam, Washington DC and Richmond.

The Western Theater was the most important theater during the Civil War, and was defined by both geography and the progression of the campaigns. It originally represented the areas east of the Mississippi River and west of the Appalachian Mountains. In 1864-1865 the area of the Western Theater extended their operations in Georgia and the Carolinas.

The Trans-Mississippi Theater ran the major military and Navy operations west of the Mississippi River, it was formed in 1862 and included Missouri, Arkansas, Texas, and the Indian territory.

1862

Military actions intensified in the Eastern and Western Theaters. Union victories in February and April helped give Union the control of Tennessee. Confederate troops began frustrated in an unsuccessful effort to gain control of Missouri in the Battle of Pea Ridge. The Confederates invaded Kentucky after the upset of the capture of New Orleans, which became the loss of their largest port, and ended in failure in the Battle of Perryville.

The year ended with heavy fighting and battles that including the battle of Stones River and Murfreesboro. These battled opened up movements in the Union to capture Vicksburg. The Confederate victories at the Seven Days Battle and the Second Bull Run pushed back a large threat to Richmond.

The year 1862 finished with the Confederacy enacting the first national conscription act, the North putting the emancipation alongside unification and with the Union facing a costly set back at Fredericksburg.

The political situation within the North and South continued to grow and intensify. The North began to modernize, developing new urban values, which was threatening to the South. The Power of the Republican Party was one signal to the South and the majority of the North had turned to a frightening revolutionary future.

While the Confederate Congress established conscription and passed taxing legislation, it failed to address many important issues. The major issues Congress conspired on was the bashing of the Davis Administration and the policies they opposed, leaving less time to concentrate of legislation for the Supreme Court and other issues, other than the override of one Presidential veto and a minor postage bill.

The Union Congress' relationship with Lincoln varied, although they did pass into law all of the important issues presented by his administrative that promoted economic growth including; a homestead bill offering land to any settlers in the west, land subsidies for the construction of a transcontinental railroad, an increase in the tariff, and grants to promote agricultural growth. However the backlash of the Emancipation Proclamation resulted in Republican losses at the polls.

SOUTHERN FEARS OF REPUBLICAN CONTROL

With the Republican Party in office following the election of Abraham Lincoln, the South feared he would make good on his promise to stop the expansion of slavery and make the steps toward the extinction of slavery. Southerners felt that even if Lincoln didn't pursue the extinction of slavery, another Northerner would soon do so. The slave states began to face a future as a perpetual minority in the house, senate and Electoral College, increasing the power of the North.

LINCOLN'S CABINET

Lincoln's cabinet was known to be a highly effective group, even though Lincoln was known to appoint political rivals to positions in his cabinet to keep them in line with his party.

1st Term Cabinet
William H. Seward, Secretary of State
Salmon P. Chase, Secretary of the Treasury
Simon Cameron, Secretary of War
Gideon Welles, Secretary of the Navy
Caleb Smith, Secretary of the Interior
Montgomery Blair, Postmaster-General
Edward Pates, Attorney-General

2nd Term Cabinet
William H. Seward, Secretary of State
Hugh McCulloch, Secretary of the Treasury
Edwin M. Stanton, Secretary of War
Gideon Welles, Secretary of the Navy
William Dennison, Postmaster-General
J. P. Usher, Secretary of the Interior
James Speed, Attorney-General

THE BEGINNING OF CONSCRIPTION

Conscription refers to an involuntary labor demanded by an established authority, yet is most often referred to specific government policies that require citizens to serve in the armed forces, today it is referred to as the draft.

Armies of the Union and the Confederate relied heavily on conscription. There was no general military draft in America until the Civil War. The Confederacy passed its first of three conscription acts on the 16th of April 1862, calling for men between the ages of 18-35. The age limit was raised in September of 1862 to include men up to the age of 45, and in February of 1864 the call of men went to all men between the ages of 17-50. Conscripted men made up one-fourth of the Confederate armies between 1864 and 1865.

Conscription through the Union began in July 1863 and then ran again in March, July and December of 1864. Names of men 18-35 were drawn through the Unions Conscription and of the 249,000 names drawn only about six percent of those men served; others either paid dues or hired a substitute. Those who lacked having a substitute or money to pay the dues were angry at the conscription and retaliated with riots throughout New York in 1863.

Those who opposed conscription felt it was a violation on individual free will and they feared that soldiers who were forced into battle would make poor fighting men and that the conscription compromised volunteer soldiers from enlisting seeing the conscription act as an act of desperation. While government officials, plagued with manpower shortages, regarded drafting as the only means of sustaining an effective army and hoped it would spur voluntary enlistments.

STATE RIGHTS

State Rights refers to the political power and Constitutional rights of a state in relation to the federal government. The concept is used to defend a state law that the federal government wants to override.

Jefferson Davis made the following argument: "The union of these States rests on the equality of rights and privileges among its members, and that it is especially the duty of the Senate, which represents the States in their sovereign capacity, to resist all attempts to discriminate either in relation to person or property, so as, in the Territories – which are the common possession of the United States – to give advantages to the citizens of one state which are not equally secured to those of every state."

Through slavery was the initial dispute leading to the Civil War, the dispute over state rights was the ultimate conflict. Southerners argued that it was the right of each state to decide on the issue of slavery and their right to exercise authority over slave property wherever it went; the Supreme Court endorsed this argument in the Dred Scott decision. Northerners in opposition to slavery indicated that the federal government held the power to govern the states as a whole and that their rights were violated by legislation like the Fugitive Slave Act.

STATE RIGHTS AND SLAVERY IN TERRITORIES

Southerners felt that the role of the federal government was strictly limited and could not abridge the rights of states as reserved in Amendment X and had no power to prevent slaves from coming into new territories. Activists of State Rights cited, in addition to the state rights, fugitive slave clauses in the Constitution to demand jurisdiction over slaves who escape to the North. Jefferson Davis, the leader chosen by the South, defined equality to be based on a state's individual population, and declared that the rights of one state (or the will of the federal government) could not supersede another. In the North, anti-slavery forces took a reverse stance. They believed Congress to be a joint agent of the states.

SOUTHERN HOPE OF EUROPEAN AID

The most important foreign relations to the United States included Europe, England and France; these countries strongly sympathized with the Confederacy. These countries had a monarchy, and they rarely liked to see the success of a rebellion land. Southerners felt that just a little intervening from one of these countries would lead to the independence of the South, and Europe was not happy with the Yankee Democracy and success. They would have been satisfied with the fall of the Union, to prove that democracy could not survive. Yet, neither Europe nor France would have been involved in fighting over the preservation of slavery, but the war became a much larger issue in the fall of 1862.

The Federal government themselves stated that they were fighting to save the Union, this only aided in the South's need for foreign aid throughout the Civil War, citing the words of the Federal Government, attempting to convince Europeans they could aid the South without fighting to aid slavery.

ARMY OF THE POTOMAC UNDER MCCLELLAN

Major General George B. McClellan took the lead position of the Army of the Potomac, and drastically changed the makeup of the army, which was the major Union Army. He was originally designated to command the Division of the Potomac, which included the Departments of Northeast Virginia and Washington. The Department of the Shenandoah merged with the army of the Potomac and on that day, July 26, 1861, the army officially became the Army of the Potomac.

In the middle of a surprise Confederate attack, McClellan was unable to repel the attacks, due to malarial fever, yet his men were successful. He still received criticism from Washington for a failure to counterattack, which they believed would have given them the ability to take over the city of Richmond. The next three weeks McClellan spent repositioning his troops, only to lose valuable time. As General Robert E. Lee command and strengthened the Army of Northern Virginia. McClellan's failure at the Peninsula Campaign forced Lincoln to appoint Major General John Pope.

WAR IN THE WEST

Even though the Confederate forces made a number of successful runs on the eastern theatre, they had great losses in the west. The war in the west was originally in the area of the Mississippi River and west of the Appalachian Mountains. As the war progressed and the Union armies moved Southeast through Chattanooga the war in the west expanded into Georgia and the Carolinas.

GENERALS GRANT, BUELL AND SHERMAN

General Grant was appointed Brigadier General, producing a first major victory for the Union with his attack on Fort Donelson. He met with an onslaught of criticism for heavy losses during a Confederate attack at Shiloh. His victory of the Battle of Chattanooga in 1864 led to his position as Commander of the Union Army, Grant also devised the stronghold on Vicksburg, which cut the Confederacy in half and was the primary overseer of the attack of General Robert E. Lee's forces bringing the war to an end.

Colonel Sherman participated in some of the Civil War's biggest campaigns including Bull Run, Shiloh, Vicksburg and Chattanooga after returning to the army in 1861 when the South seceded. He was the commander of the Union Armies of the Cumberland driving incredible serge against the armies of General Joseph E. Johnston, which ended the Union's occupation of Atlanta. His strategies included the psychological intimidation and an economical cripple to intimidate the rebels. Other campaigns included his "March to the Sea" that ended with the occupation of Savannah and the march through the Carolinas where he received Johnston's surrender.

General Buell was an early organizer of the Army of the Potomac. In 1861, he was appointed as the head of the Department of Ohio for operations in eastern Tennessee. He was promoted to Major General of Volunteers.

NAVAL INVOLVEMENT

The Navy was an important factor of the outcome of the Civil War. The Navy launched a series of successful assault actions that sealed off blockade-runners and blockading ships from getting to their bases in the Southern Coast. Though it was not complete, control of the sea by the Union Navy isolated the South, giving the Northern military an added dimension of mobility.

BLOCKAGE AND BLOCKAGE RUNNERS

Blockades were massive naval actions that were set up on the Atlantic Ocean and the Gulf Coast designed to prevent the passage of trade goods, supplies and armor for the Confederacy. The Blockade was originally conspired by Union General Winfield Scott as inspired by the Anaconda Plan, to win the war with as little bloodshed as possible. Winfield thought if the Union blocked the main ports it would eventually strangle the Confederate's economy and force them to surrender. In 1861, Lincoln proclaimed all Southern ports were to be under the Union Blockade, to immediately shut down all international shipping to the Confederate ports. He required the closure of 3,500 miles of

Confederate coastline, which included New Orleans, Louisiana and Mobile, Alabama. These were the top cotton-exporting ports before the Civil War began. The women of Mobile, Alabama were so angry about there not being enough bread to feed their families that they rioted. They carried banners and demanded bread that they were denied because of the blockade. Lincoln commissioned some 500 actions that would ultimately destroy 1,500 blockade-runners throughout the time of war.

GENERAL LEE

General Lee had no sympathy with secession or slavery and condemned the thought of sectional conflict. His loyalty to Virginia came first and when Virginia's secession was final he resigned from the Federal Army. Lee assumed command of the military and naval forces of Virginia. Lee took leadership of the Army of the Northern Virginia in June 1862 when his next three years in this role would land him among the world's greatest leaders.

GENERAL JACKSON

Jackson was a Brigadier General in the Confederate Army, where he and his army would be considered to be "like a stone wall" at the first battle of Bull Run and he came to be known as Stonewall Jackson. He was promoted to Major General in November of 1861 and was assigned to command Shenandoah Valley. Jackson fought in the seven-day battles and the Antietam alongside of General Lee. After the war of the Antietam, Lee was promoted to Lieutenant General. He commanded the Confederate's right to battle of Fredericksburg and Chancellorsville, where the fire of his own men fatally wounded Jackson. His death was a terrible blow to the Southern cause and he soon became a figurehead of the Civil War.

 # Major Battles

The major battles of 1862 throughout the Eastern Civil War took place in various locations and have come to be known by the names that follow; Shiloh, the Second Manassas, Antietam, and Fredericksburg.

SHILOH

The Battle of Shiloh followed the attack of Grant's Army from Johnston's Army on April 6, 1862 on the landing of the Tennessee River. The battle forced the Union to move back on the second day. With 13,000 of soldiers lost from the Federals and 10,700 men out of the Confederates the total losses were shocking. While Grant was accused of lacking elementary caution from the North, the South was morning the loss of Johnston.

SECOND MANASSAS

The failure of the Peninsular Campaign was a letdown to the Lincoln administration and Lincoln soon named Henry W. Halleck as the General-In-Chief of the Union Armies. The Army of Virginia was organized and commanded by General John Pope. This new Army was attacked August 1862 by the troops of Jackson. Over 23,000 troops surrounded Pope's Army. Jackson then captured and destroyed supplies and made a stand at Manassas. Ultimately Pope was thoroughly beaten, losing a total of 14,500 men, while Lee only lost 9,200. This led to Pope's Army merged with McClellan, who led the entire force.

ANTIETAM

The bloodiest one-day battle in American history has come to be known in the United States as the Battle of Antietam. Although Lee did not feel he would be completely successful, he decided to invade and attack Washington. Lee moved his troops across the Potomac River while sending most of his army out to Harpers Ferry. Lee stationed the rest of his army up at Sharpsburg, near Antietam Creek.

Once the fighting began on September 17, the Confederate Army held off the large number of Union forces. Just as Union General Ambrose Burnside detained a bridge and led his men across the river, A.P. Hill brought reinforcements. The Union attack was restrained and the fighting stopped while Lee led his men back to Virginia. About 12,500 Union casualties' lives were lost, while 10,500 Confederates died.

Peninsular Campaign

At Fort Monroe on the Southeastern tip of the peninsula, McClellan arrived with over 100,000 men. They eventually took the town of Yorktown after a month's siege, but ultimately allowed the Confederate defenders to escape. Confederate General Joseph Johnston attempted to stop McClellan and his men, yet he was unsuccessful and was wounded in the battle. Robert E Lee replaced Johnston as commander of the Army of Northern Virginia, giving him respect from the South and fear from the North. Not long after his appointment a variety of battles took place, known as the Seven Days Battle, began.

The day after those battles began, Union General Fitz-John Porter drove back a Confederate attack on Mechanicsville, northeast of Richmond. Instead of pushing onwards,

McClellan withdrew, ordering Porter to fall back to Gaines's Mill. Setting his sights on Harrison's Landing, McClellan and his men found guard actions at Savage's Station, Frayser's Farm, and Malvern Hill, and finally reached Harrison's Landing on the last day. The Peninsular Campaign was over with losses that totaled 16,000 Union casualties and 20,000 of Robert E. Lee's men. This win is ironic because if Lee had lost, the South would have been likely to keep their slaves for a while longer.

MONITOR VS. MERRIMAC

The USS Monitor was the first Ironclad warship, before 1862 all warships were made primarily of wood. The USS Merrimac was a screw frigate, best known as "The Hulk." The USS Monitor and the USS Merrimac met at the Battle of Hampton Roads, also called the Battle of the Monitor and the Battle of the Merrimac. The battle was famous for being the first fight between two iron-covered warships.

The Navy battle lasted for two days. On the second day of battle the Monitor initiated the famous action that is known as the Duel of the Ironclads. Although the battle was inconclusive, it was significant to naval warfare and dramatically changed the way ships were made.

FREDERICKSBURG

On the hills near Fredericksburg, Virginia, just south of the Rappahannock River, troops lead by Ambrose E. Burnside, the new commander of the Army of the Potomac, engaged in strong defensive positions. The result was another slaughter; killing 12,600 Union soldiers while the Confederate soldiers lost only 5,300 soldiers.

Unsatisfied with another commander for the Army of the Potomac, Lincoln relieved Burnside of his position and appointed Joseph Hooker.

1863

The beginning of 1863 looked grim for the Northern military, the west's effort to capture Vicksburg remained a frustration, and the Union forces were defeated in Chancellorsville. The Union adopted a national conscription act, which prompted worldwide opposition and added to the uproar of violence.

Critics of the war organized Peace Democrats, opposition sparked due to huge casualty lists, civil rights violations, emancipations, wartime failures and the draft. Copperheads is the name of the group that wanted an immediate end to the war and they made major electoral gains in 1862 and almost won the governess of Ohio in 1863.

The Emancipation Proclamation went into effect at the beginning of January, when the North began to recruit black soldiers, while shortages of food and supplies became severe to the Confederacy.

EMANCIPATION PROCLAMATION

The Emancipation Proclamation was an order that declared the freedom of all slaves in the areas of the Confederate States of America, which had not already claimed to Union control. Abraham Lincoln ordered the Proclamation in 1863. It was not so much a law passed by Congress, but more a Presidential order empowered by his Commander In Chief of the Army and Navy position.

The Emancipation Proclamation only affected to the already freed slaves at first, but as the armies conquered the South, thousands of slaves were freed. Nearly all slaves were free by July 1865 and the number of free slaves increased until the entire institution was eradicated by the thirteenth Amendment in December 1865.

ANTI-EMANCIPATION SENTIMENT

The Emancipation Proclamation received hostilities in several sections of the North and within some parts of the Union Army. Copperheads had no desire to extend the benefits of Americans to African-Americans. Their racist attitude would continue to trouble race relations in the Midwest for years to come.

CASUALTIES

The Union suffered a blow of losing 110,000 soldiers who were killed in action with a total number of soldiers dead of 360,000 and another 275,200 soldiers injured. The Confederates numbers were lower with 93,000 soldiers killed in the line of duty, 258,000 total deaths and over 137,000 wounded.

CAUSES OF CASUALTIES

Soldiers in the Civil War had more to worry about than just the battles they endured, disease was the biggest killer of soldiers in the Civil War. An estimated three out of five soldiers died from disease. Half of the soldiers that died from disease were caused from typhoid fever, diarrhea and dysentery, while the remainder died from pneumonia and tuberculosis.

Many of the cramped camps were exposed to outbreaks of the measles, chickenpox, mumps and the whooping cough. Not only were the camps filled with diseases they were in a state of failed conditions, littered with offensive garbage that were in a state of decomposition. This fueled bacteria and viruses to grow; in fact an estimated 995 soldiers out of 1,000 eventually contracted some type of diarrhea or dysentery.

CARE OF WOUNDED AND SICK

During the time of the Civil War little was known about the causes of diseases and how to stop them. Even surgical techniques ranged from the barbaric to barely competent. Wounded soldiers had a one in four chance of death. The medical staff at the beginning of the war were unqualified, understaffed and barely had enough supplies to meet the demands of the wounded soldiers.

Every effort was made to care for the wounded within forty-eight hours of their calamity, they were transported to field hospitals far behind the line of war. Many soldiers whose limbs were damaged beyond repair had to have their legs and/or arms amputated. Although it has been known that soldiers who were amputated did not receive anesthetic, the truth is victims received ample amounts of chloroform. Because of these misconceptions however, the soldiers and the media considered war doctors as butchers. During the time of the war nearly 30,000 soldiers had to have an extremity amputated.

Yet amputation did not mean those soldiers were safe, there was still a very high risk of infections. Although most surgeons were aware of the low rate of infections with cleanliness, many were not aware of procedures of sterilizing their equipment and sometimes went days without washing their hands or their instruments.

Throughout the few years the war went on the South and the North struggled to improve the care given to fallen soldiers. The medical industry made large advances throughout and after the Civil War and doctors began to understand the relationship of cleanliness, diet and disease and the use of anesthesia.

PRISONERS OF WAR

At the beginning of the war prisoners were exchanged on the battlefield, a private for a private, sergeant for a sergeant, a captain for a captain, until 1862 with the creation of large holding pens for POW's. Major General John A. Dix of the Union Army met with Confederate representative Major General Daniel Hill. A cartel was drafted for the parole and exchange of prisoners, approved by superiors and formally signed after four days and became known as the Dix-Hill Cartel. Mid-year the cartel failed due to the refusal of the Confederates to exchange black prisoners.

The Secretary of War, Edwin M. Stanton, directed that there would no longer be more exchanges. This decision greatly increased the size of Northern and Southern prison camps. Both sides used more than 150 places during the war to house prisoners, such as the Confederacy's Castle Pinckney and the Unions Fort Warren, Fort Lafayette, Fort McHenry and Fort Delaware.

ROLE OF WOMEN IN WAR

Although records of the woman who served during the Civil War are very limited, an estimated two thousand women volunteered. Most women, however, sought out more conventional ways to help and served as volunteer nurses in the military hospitals. Some of the influential woman who recorded their experience for posterity included Louisa May Walcott, Katherine Prescott Wormeley and Jane Stuart Woolsey. The introduction of female personnel within the military hospitals made a notable impact on the men they cared for those they served under, as well as having a significant step toward larger roles for woman in American society.

Two other prominent women, Dorothea Dix and Clara Barton, led the national effort to organize a nursing corps for the war's wounded and sick soldiers. Dix recruited woman to serve as nurses in the Army Medical Bureau, although military traditionalists opposed her. She was noted for making major strides in the treatment for the insane.

Clara Barton played a major role in the care for the wounded soldiers that returned to Washington DC. She received a pass from General William Hammond to ride in Army ambulances. Eventually, she was given permission to travel behind the lines and administer to the wounded on the battlefield. She became known as the "angel of the battlefield." She also became a major participant in the creation of the American branch of the International Red Cross.

BLACK AMERICANS AND THE WAR

For most of the war the Confederate Government prohibited the enlistment of African Americans in the military; however both runaway slaves and free African Americans alike served totaling 163 units of African Americans served in the Union Army. The most widely known incident featuring African American soldiers was the assault on Fort Wagner, South Carolina by the 54th Massachusetts Volunteer Infantry - one of the first official black unit in the United States. Nearly 180,000 African Americans served in the Union Army and the Union Navy during the Civil War.

With the confederacy losing ground and battles, Robert E. Lee wrote the Confederate Congress urging them to enlist black slaves in exchange for their freedom. President Davis signed the order in March 1865.

Some individual states in the confederacy allowed free blacks to enlist, the first state being Tennessee who passed a law in 1861 authorizing their recruitment. It wasn't until July of 1862 that Congress passed two acts allowing African-Americans to enlist in the military, calling into action the recruitment of "free persons of color" between the ages of 15-50 to serve in the war.

Louisiana followed suit and formed the all-black 1st Louisiana Native Guard, although the regiment was forced to disband due to legislature passing and the new conscription calling for "all the free white males capable of bearing arms."

RUNAWAY SLAVES

Many slaves in the South escaped to freedom, within the Free states, through safety routes such as the Underground Railroad, the Mississippi River, while others fled to bordering states. A network of safe houses, contact points and freedom operations were conducted and offered for those slaves who found freedom.

Southern slaveholders, attempting to stop slaves from escaping, enforced strict laws for slaves who sought freedom; this became the Compromise of 1850. Northerners fought back by holding group meetings and events where they presented a free black to portray the horrors of slavery.

POLITICAL SITUATION

The North grew dissatisfied with President Lincoln, with the battle loses had been staggering and Grant hadn't taken Richmond or destroyed Lee's army. Northern politicians began scouting for another Presidential election. Republicans complained of Lincoln being too easygoing in the prosecution of the war and too moderate on the slavery issue, while the Democrats believed the South would not be defeated and wanted a peaceful end to the war at all costs.

NORTH

Gettysburg and Vicksburg were the most important victories for the Union in two years of war. With the start of the war many Northerners were opposed to some of Lincoln's measures and they coincided with disloyal outbursts of violence in the North over the war. The Emancipation Proclamation angered those who were willing to fight for the Union, but not for the abolition of slavery, while other Northerners grew weary of a war they could see no end to and wanted the end to the war.

CONSCRIPTION IN 1863

In March of 1863 the first conscription act was passed because of recruiting difficulties. The order was for all men between the ages of 20-45 to be called for military services. The only way to avoid the order was to pay a fee or to get a substitute. This was seen as unfair to the poor and working class individuals who could not pay for a substitute.

Officials attempted to put the draft into effect in New York City, but was met with an angry mob, made up of mostly poor immigrants most of which were of Irish decent.

The mob attacked the draft headquarters, setting fire to it and other residential and business buildings with four days of fighting between the mob, local police, fire and military causing more than $1.5 million dollars of damage and destruction. The troops from the Army of the Potomac rushed in and restored order. Other parts of the country met with opposition over conscription, but none compared to the riots in New York.

COPPERHEADS

Peace Democrats from the North, often referred to as Copperheads, opposed the Civil War and the Lincoln administration. During the Civil War the Copperheads favored the Union while strongly opposing the war, demanding peace and resisting the draft laws. They wanted Lincoln and the Republicans out of office feeling that Lincoln was destroying American Republican values with his arbitrary actions. Many Copperheads attempted to persuade the Union soldiers to desert, while they talked of helping Confederates seize camps and help them escape.

INFLATION

To help finance the war, Congress and the Confederacy both issued paper money. Inflation followed, peaking in 1864, it dropped sharply after the war ended. On the eve of the Civil War the price level in the United States was twenty-eight percent below that of the 1800's, which served long-term deflation in the economy.

The Confederate government was not the only one issuing money in the South. States, counties, cities, and private businesses also issued their own money. This process encouraged for the counterfeit of money in the South, giving the South runaway inflation.

The collapse of the currency came with the loss of the war, after the war the confederacy ended in a complete loss of value of Confederate issues and exacerbated the burdens of the war.

SHORTAGES

In a letter written by General Lee he stated that he depended greatly on blockade-runners to supply shoes, blankets and leather for the winter. Southerners supplies and food had been exceptionally low through 1862 and 1863.

One of the main reasons for the low supply of food in the South was poor distribution. The railroads were in pitiable shape and had poor management. The shortage of meat was extremely high due to the Fall of Vicksburg and the minimal communication with the trans-Mississippi department. By November of 1863, pounds of meat, food, supplies and other essentials made it to the South from the Confederacy government.

BREAD RIOT IN RICHMOND

As the war entered its third year, things were looking desperate in many parts of the South. Heavy inflation and blockades by the North had cut off the city of Richmond from necessary food and supplies. This was also the time when the war began turning in favor of the Union Army. As a result, many Southerners began to lose hope. A group of women in Richmond decided to band together and demand food from the Governor, but when they arrived they were told that he was too busy to meet with them. The women refused to be discouraged and began to riot through the city. They broke windows in shops and stole beef, bacon, bread, and jewelry in their desperation. Soon the Governor, along with Jefferson Davis, was in the streets trying to calm the crowd. The women eventually dispersed, and although a few were arrested, they were released not long afterwards because the prisons couldn't afford to feed them. Despite efforts to ensure that news of the riot wouldn't spread, it was the front page story in many prominent newspapers a week later. It became a sign of the desperation of the South, and built morale among Union members.

 # Major Battles

CHANCELLORSVILLE

The Union Army crossed the Rappahannock River on April 27, 1863 beginning the Chancellorsville Campaign. Heavy fighting began on May 1st and did not end until the Union forces retreated across the river on May 5, 1863. The Union brought with them 133,868 men onto the field. The Confederate army had less than half of that, standing at 60,892.

The soldiers fought under terrible conditions. Fires started throughout the course of the battle and the soldiers got lost in the overgrown weeds. Despite being outnumbered General Lee won, arguably his greatest victory, but not without a great loss of over 13,000 casualties.

CHICKAMAUGA

The Battle of Chickamauga, named for the Chickamauga Creek, was the most significant Union defeat in the Civil War. It marked the end of a Union offensive in south-central Tennessee and northwestern Georgia. The battle was fought between the Union of the Cumberland and the Confederate Army of Tennessee.

Rosecrans, Commander of the Army of the Cumberland, withdrew his forces to the city of Chattanooga, while Confederates occupied surrounding heights and laid siege upon the Union forces. The battle claimed 34,624 soldier casualties, 16,170 Union members and 18,454 Confederate members.

CHATTANOOGA

The Battle of Chattanooga, also known as the Third Battle of Chattanooga (which included the battle of Chattanooga, the Battle of Lookout Mountain and the Battle of the Missionary Ridge) eliminated the last Confederate control of Tennessee and opened the door to an invasion of the Deep South that led to the Atlanta Campaign of 1864.

STONES RIVER (MURFREESBORO)

In the Western theatre of the Civil War the Battle of Stones River or Second Battle of Murfreesboro was fought. The battle began on December of 1862 and ended on January 1863 in Middle Tennessee.

VICKSBURG

The final significant battle of the Civil War in the Western Theater was the Battle of the Vicksburg or Siege of Vicksburg. The Army of the Tennessee under the Union's Major General Ulysses S. Grant crossed the Mississippi and drove the Confederate army into defensive lined at Vicksburg, Mississippi. The city of Vicksburg surrendered six weeks later giving Grant command of the Mississippi River to the Union.

GETTYSBURG

The Battle of the Gettysburg was the bloodiest battle of the American Civil War and is often said to have been the turning point. It was a three-day battle in the town of Gettysburg, Pennsylvania. The two armies collided on July 1st. While the Union defended the low ridges to the Northwest of town with two corps of Union infantries, two large Confederate corps assaulted them from the Northwest and North. This collapsed the Union lines sending them through the streets of town and to the hills.

Lee launched a heavy assault on the Union and fierce fighting raged the Union defenders held their lines, despite significant losses. A dramatic assault by 12,500 Confederates against the center of the Union line was defended with great success, the Confederate army lost significantly. Nearly 51,000 Americans were casualties in the three-day battle that ended on July 3rd. President Lincoln used the ceremony, Gettysburg National Cemetery to honor those Union soldiers who had lost their lives and to offer his Gettysburg Address.

1864 to May 1865

The year 1864 began optimistically for the North, expecting Grant to bring victory. Grant planned an aggressive campaign. In the summer of 1864 both the armies under Grant and Sherman began to bog down as Confederate Jubal Early threatened Washington making it apparent to Lincoln that he would not win a reelection. The Democratic Party nominated General George B. McClellan for President. But when the war turned his way, as Sheridan defeated Early and Sherman captured Atlanta, overwhelming support of the Union soldiers and the Union party Lincoln swept the election.

POLITICAL SITUATION

While the failure of Davis to maintain productive relations with state governments damaged Confederacies ability to draw on regional resources, the Union's executive branch allowed a streamlined conduct of the war. The Republicans were able to support the troops, even when the war became unpopular, through a strong party system. The Confederates deliberately did not use parties; their failure to win diplomatic or military support cut them off from access to markets and most imports.

SHERMAN'S MARCH THROUGH GEORGIA

The Savannah Campaign was commonly known as Sherman's March to the Sea, pursued in 1864 by Major General William Tecumseh Sherman of the Union Army. Sherman's troops left Atlanta, Georgia after capturing it and marched on to capture the port of Savannah on December 22, 1864.

GENERAL JOHNSTON

Confederate President Jefferson Davis considered General Albert Johnston the finest General in the Confederacy. In the outbreak of the Civil War Johnston was the commander of the US Army Department of the Pacific in California, where he resigned his commission once he heard of Texas's secession. After he marched through Arizona and Texas and reached Virginia in September of 1861 he accepted the second highest ranking of a Confederate general as the commander of the Western Department.

He raised the Army of the Mississippi to defend Confederate lines. Johnston died in battle at the Battle of Shiloh.

GENERAL FORREST

Forrest came to be known as on the highest regarded cavalry and partisan ranger, he was known as the one of the war's most successful generals. He was a Confederate Army general and an instrumental figure in the founding growth of the Ku Klux Klan.

LEE AND THE ARMY OF NORTHERN VIRGINIA

General Lee served as a soldier in the U.S. Army for thirty-two years. His first major role in the U.S. Army was in 1862 when he commanded the Army of Northern Virginia, which was the primary Confederate military force in the Eastern Theater. Yet, in early 1861 Lee opposed the formation of the Confederacy, until his home state of Virginia seceded from the Union.

Although both of Lee's campaigns to invade the North failed, he had great victories including the Seven Days Battle, the Battle of Chancellorsville, the Battle of the Fredericksburg, and the Second Battle of Bull Run. Lee barely escaped the Battle of Gettysburg when flooded waters cut off his escape routes.

Lee lost heavy casualties during the Overland Campaign and the siege of Petersburg; he was forced to abandon the Confederate capital of Richmond and was forced to surrender at Appomattox. While his victories won him fame and became the great Southern hero of the war, many of his losses created much criticism.

Major Battles

The major battles of 1864 included the Wilderness, Spotsylvania, Cold Harbor, Shenandoah Valley, Petersburg, Lee's continued March through and the Fall of Richmond. A separate campaign launched by General Sherman included the Battle of Atlanta and Mobile Bay, which resulted in the shutdown of two remaining Confederate ports.

In a joint campaign to crush Lee, Grant and Hood joined together with the Army of the Potomac. An expedition was sent against Fort Fisher at the Cape Fear River in North Carolina, but the Fort fell. The loss deprived the Confederacy of its stronghold, which tightened the Union Blockade. It sealed the port of Wilmington, North Carolinas only leaving Galveston, Texas open to blockade-runners.

ATLANTA

The Battle of Atlanta began in July 1864 just Southeast of Atlanta Georgia, the city fought for six weeks. Major General William Sherman was commander of the Union forces in the Western Theater, while the main force in the Battle of the Atlanta was led by James B. McPherson, which was Sherman and Grant's favorite commander, and the Army of Tennessee. The Battle raged against the Confederate Army of Tennessee General John Bell Hood, while Lieutenant General William J. Hardee led the attack.

Hood's army held the city, while Sherman sent raids west and south to cut off supply lines from Georgia. In only two days Hood pulled his troops out of Atlanta destroying the supply depots as he left. Sherman ordered the evacuation of all troops, while he and his army burned the town to the ground, departing east on what would become Sherman's March to the Sea.

MOBILE BAY

The Union forces initiated operations to close Mobile Bay to blockade-runners. Eighteen Union ship fleets entered Mobile Bay and received devastating fire from Forts Gaines and Morgan. The Confederate Naval forces surrendered, effectively closing Mobile Bay. The Battle of Mobile Bay was a significant boost to Abraham Lincoln's reelection. The battle successfully shut down two remaining Confederate ports.

WILDERNESS

The Battle of the Wilderness was the first battle of Ulysses S. Grant in 1864 Virginia, the Overland Campaign, against Robert E. Lee. Both armies lost many soldiers during the battle that took place from May 5th through May 7th 1864.

SPOTSYLVANIA

Between 1862 and 1864 the second Battle with Ulysses S. was the Battle of the Spotsylvania Court House, also referred as the Battle of Spotsylvania, which was fought on the Rapidan-Rappahannock River in Virginia. Both sides lost more than 100,000 men during the battle.

COLD HARBOR

The Battle of Cold Harbor was the final battle fought under Ulysses S. Grant during the American Civil War. It is remembered as one of American Histories bloodiest campaigns. Grant has been quoted as saying of the war, "I have always regretted that the last assault at Cold Harbor was ever made. I might say the same thing of the assault of the May, 22 1863, at Vicksburg. At Cold Harbor no advantage whatever was gained to compensate for the heavy loss we sustained." Thousands of Union soldiers lost their lives during the battles that took place.

SHENANDOAH VALLEY CAMPAIGN

Jubal Anderson Early was sent by Lee to operate in the Shenandoah Valley and to wreak havoc on Washington, a campaign that was hoped to force Grant's grip on Petersburg. Early and his troops defeated several Union armies, including Monocracy, yet the battle held Early up and forces in Washington were able to reinforce. Early was able to get close to outskirts of Washington when he sent his men to the west side of Washington as his infantry attacked at Fort Stevens.

Grant began to lose patience with Early and realized that Washington was vulnerable with Early in command. Grant sent in Phillip Sheradon, commander of the Army of the Potomac, calling them now the Army of the Shenandoah.

The following battles were fought with the Shenandoah Valley; Battle of Guard Hill (August 16), Battle of Summit Point (August 21), Battle of Smithfield Crossing (August 25- 29), Battle of Berryville (September 3-4), Battle of Opequon (September 19), Battle of Fisher's Hill (September 21-22), Battle of Tom's Brook (October 9), and Battle of Cedar Creek (October 9).

Those battle weakened Early's troops from the valley as well as devastating the area to the extent that the farms couldn't send food and supplies to Lee's troops. Many of Early's troops joined Lee at Petersburg, leaving Early to command a skeleton army. After his final defeat at the Battle of Waynesboro. Lee relieved Early of his duties.

PETERSBURG

The siege of Petersburg, also known as the Richmond-Petersburg Campaign, was not like many of the classic military sieges throughout the American Civil War where the city was fully surrounded and supply lines cut off. The siege of Petersburg consisted of ten months filled with trench warfare where Grant constructed trench lines over thirty miles around the outskirts of the city.

In retaliation Grant attempted to cross the James River, circle around Lee's army and Confederate capital to Petersburg and fall in a sudden attack on Richmond from the South before Lee could come to its defense. The attack almost succeeded until the Confederate realized Grant's plan and managed to stop his advance on Petersburg, where heavy fighting occurred from June 15th through June 18th. Grant was unable to endure the assault; he prepared to starve the city into surrendering. Almost a year later the Confederate forces were on the verge of collapsing.

The Richmond-Petersburg campaign was costly for both sides, an estimated 42,000 Union soldiers were lost and 28,000 Confederates.

SHERMAN'S CONTINUED MARCH THROUGH THE SOUTH

Sherman was convinced that the only way to end the war was to crush the Confederacy's strategies, economically and psychologically. He used scorched earth tactics to break the rebellion's backbone. Similar scorched earth policies were used in many major wars throughout the world. The tactic is to destroy everything that might be of any use to the enemy. Throughout the course of Sherman's March his men destroyed factories, bridges, railroads and public buildings in a path of three hundred miles in length and sixty miles in width.

Sherman's advance through Georgia and South Carolina devastated Southern civilian supplies and infrastructure. The speed and efficiency with which Sherman's army destroyed the land was remarkable, even though Government officials forbade looting. One of Sherman's trademark signatures was the railroad rails he bent around trees; these would come to be called Sherman's Neckties. Sherman's "neckties" made it extremely difficult to repair the areas he marched through.

 # The End of the War

FALL OF RICHMOND

Grant planned to cut off the two railroads that continued to supply the Confederates and to extend his lines west around Richmond and Petersburg. In March Lee moved his troops in to counter the threat. Sheridan defeated a Confederate force led by Pickett on April 1st, just west of Petersburg, capturing many prisoners and artillery. Lee sent three brigades to Pickett's support and decided to evacuate Richmond. Grant ordered a general assault after learning of Lee's wakened defense, his defenders resisted that gave Lee to make a withdrawal.

Lee hoped to join Johnston, who was located in North Carolina, to at least prolong the struggle. Grant was focused on preventing the two armies from uniting. Between April 3rd-17th to Confederate forces and Union forces engaged in a series of running fights. Sheridan managed to keep his brigade across the line of Lee's retreat at Appomattox Court House. Grant offered Lee, who was aware of his desperate situation with Grant's troops surrounding his, an invitation to surrender. On the Morning of April 9th the war was over in Virginia.

LEE'S SURRENDER

The South began to run out of manpower and the issue of arming slaves became important. The Confederate army was growing smaller due to casualties' disease and desertion. As Lee put the first units of black slaves to training the Union attacked at

Petersburg in 1865. Lee abandoned Richmond and retreated West, Lee surrendered himself and his army to Grant.

Upon his capture Lee stated, "So far from the engaging in a war to perpetuate slavers, I am rejoiced that slavery is abolished. I believe it will be greatly for the interests of the South."

ASSASSINATION OF LINCOLN

Abraham Lincoln was assassinated while attending a performance at Ford's theatre with his wife; he died the following day in the home of William Peterson. On the same day Secretary of State William H. Seward was attacked, but he survived. Confederate John Wilkes Booth who solely executed the assassination of Abraham Lincoln on April 14, 1865 planned both attacks. Although Booth also planned on taking out the Vice President Andrew Johnson, the man he hired to assassinate him did not go through with the plan.

Booth had hoped to cause the downfall of the Federal Government by assassinating Lincoln, Seward and Andrew Johnson.

END OF THE CONFEDERACY

Once Richmond fell to Union forces, the Confederate government collapsed. They had been hampered with constitutional limitations and their attempts were hugely unpopular, including issuing paper currency, which brought on the onset of inflation, seeking loans and selling government bonds, which barely brought in any profit and passing taxes that were unaccepted.

Davis and most of his cabinet fled South by train, taking with them the remainder of the country's treasury. Davies was captured outside of Irwinville, Georgia putting an end to the Confederate nation.

JOHNSTON'S SURRENDER

Johnston briefly gained tactical success at the Battle of Bentonville in March 1865, but large numbers of Sherman's troops forced him to retreat. Upon learning of General Lee's surrender Johnston surrendered his Army to General Sherman at Bennett Place, dismissing all orders on the contrary.

DAVIS'S CAPTURE

In May 1865, in Washington, Georgia President Jefferson Davis met for the last time with the Confederate Cabinet, upon their official disbursement. Just five days later

Davis was captured at Irwinville, Georgia and was held for two years in Fort Monroe, Virginia.

 # Cost of the War

The Confederates or the Union never anticipated the war to last as long or cost as much in soldiers' lives, destruction of property, or monetary value. Benefits from the Civil War for veterans' compensation and care for the wounded exceeded, totaling $3.3 million, the amount it cost for the Civil War altogether.

DESTRUCTION OF THE SOUTH'S CIVILIAN BASE

The South was completely devastated by the war; plantations were in complete shambles, hundreds of thousands of dollars in the value of slaves had been wiped out by the Emancipation Proclamation, banks and the capital within them were useless, factories were dismantled, and most structures all together, business and personal, had crumbled.

In the aftermath of Sherman's March, South Carolina was like a black streak of ruin and desolation. The damage created by Sherman's march was almost completely limited to the destruction of property; Sherman's strategy was total warfare in the conclusion of the Civil War.

Many of the people within the Southern states and cities including Colombia, Atlanta, Richmond, the Tennessee valley and Mobile had no homes. Transportation before the war was primitive to begin, and after the war transportation was scarce at best.

HUMAN

The human cost of the war was enormous; it had exceeded the amount anyone could have imagined. The North had nearly two million men who served in the North, of which 640,000 were killed or wounded in battle or died from some type of disease while serving. The Confederate forces were difficult to estimate, but it is believed to be close to 450,000 soldiers died out of the total of Confederates who served in the confederacy 850,000.

Without proportion from battlefield deaths to deaths from disease, making a combined total number of deaths were estimated at around 1.1 million. More Americans were killed in the Civil War than any other war from that time period until 2001.

ECONOMIC

More the a half a billion dollars' worth of property, including slavery, had been lost throughout the Civil War. All property including public buildings, railroads, steamboats, factories, farms (farm stock, buildings, and equipment), banks and capital, and mills were partially or completely destroyed.

In the South there was little supply of money and crops also failed, which were poor for years after the war. Just the bare essentials of life were slim and many people died of starvation, state authorities reported that 139,000 whites were suffering, just three months later that number rose to 200,000. With the loss of soldiers throughout the South it was reported 80,000 woman and children were without husbands or fathers.

CULTURAL

The aftermath of the Civil War changed the lives of American citizens in every possible way. Woman began to take on larger responsibilities in the workplace, due to so many of the men absent during and after the war. Northern woman performed, formerly male occupations, such as nurses, government clerks, and factory workers, while still tending to their families and the war efforts.

While Southern woman took the responsibility to tend to the farms, thousands of woman dressed like men to serve in the military alongside their brothers, fathers, and spouses, many of which were wounded during the war.

The almost four million slave men and woman found the biggest change out of the Civil War, after which they had been free, yet they would still have many years to have equal rights.

 Reconstruction

Reconstruction issues emerged early on in the war and increased with importance as Northern victories continued. Upon the control of large areas of the South by the Union forces commanders and federal government officials were forced to make decisions on how those areas should be administered.

Reconstruction began in the middle of the war and ended in 1877, creating complex changes of the federal and state policies. Reconstruction addressed the issues of the return of the South, African-American freedom, the status of ex-Confederate leaders, and the constitution. Reconstruction came in three eras, the Presidential Reconstruction (1863-1866), Radical Reconstruction (1866-1873), and Redemption (1873-1877).

Reconstruction was conducted and ended at different times per state, the last three by the Compromise of 1877. Three Civil War amendments that were added to the constitution became the long-term result of reconstruction; these three amendments abolished slavery, extended federal legal protection to citizens regardless of race and abolish racial restrictions on voting.

Controversy on how to integrate the Freedmen into the legal, political, economic and social society arose and by the late 1870's reconstruction failed.

PRESIDENTIAL RECONSTRUCTION PLANS

Presidential reconstruction was controlled by the Presidents Abraham Lincoln and Andrew Johnson. Yet, reconstruction remained undetermined when the war ended. To complicate matters Abraham Lincoln was assassinated in April of 1865 and Andrew Johnson made it clear that he did not share in the Republican Commitment in remaking the South. Johnson pursued a policy of leniency toward former rebels and one of neglect toward former slaves. Johnson offered amnesty to those who would be willing to take the oath of allegiance, except for those with a post-war wealth of over twenty thousand dollars, who had to apply for a pardon directly to Johnson personally. He also, in coordination with these pardons, reversed General Sherman's Special Field Order No. 15 and ordered that all abandoned plantations be returned to their former owners.

Johnson sought to restore political rights to Southern states and for each state he appointed a governor who was required to call a constitutional convention that would draft a new constitution outlawing slavery and disavowing secession. Southern whites reorganized according to Johnson's plan and passed a series of plans, known as black codes; to restrict the rights of frees slaves. The codes varied from state to state, but basically included vagrancy laws, limitations on black occupations and property holdings, and children without proper care could be bound out to while employees.

ABRAHAM LINCOLN

Lincoln began the task of reconstruction in 1863, he was motivated by a need to build a strong Republican party in the South and end the bitterness between the North and the South. He issued a proclamation of amnesty and reconstruction in the area the Confederacy occupied by the Union Armies. Although Lincoln pursued a plan for reconstruction of Virginia Louisiana, Tennessee, and Arkansas, he could not get the support for his plans from Congress.

JOHNSON

Northerners became exceedingly angry over the assassination of Lincoln and the reality of the loss of life from the Civil War, they demanded harsh policies. But Johnson took on softer consequences, pardoning many Confederate leaders and allowed ex-Confederates to maintain control of the South, including governments, lands and black people.

He quickly put into action the "Black Codes," which were laws that constricted civil rights and civil liberties of blacks, especially freed slaves. While the black codes outraged Northern opinions and the South feared black vagrancy, the codes had little effect and were overthrown by the Civil Rights Act of 1866.

While Andrew Johnson attempted to veto all Civil Rights acts, his vetoes were overturned and eventually his rebellion to civil rights led him to being impeached in 1868.

CONGRESSIONAL RECONSTRUCTION PLANS

In March of 1865 Congress adjourned to leave matters of reconstruction in the hands of President Lincoln and Johnson, so when they met up in December of that year a recess of eight months to carry out their plans. Congress appointed a committee of fifteen, nine representatives and six senators; their immediate responsibility was to look into the condition of the seceded states and to advise congress.

RADICAL REPUBLICANS

A fraction of American politicians took a hard line against the Confederacy throughout the war and opposed Lincoln's "too easy" terms for reuniting the nation. The Radical Republicans supported federal civil rights and allowed free slaves to vote in the South, all except ex-Confederates. They demanded that a more aggressive prosecution of the war and faster destruction of slavery gave them the fuel to fight moderate Republicans such as the President Abraham Lincoln, then his successor Andrew Johnson who they fought to impeach.

During the end of the war the Radicals were led by Thaddeus Stevens in the house and Charles Sumner in the Senate, in 1868 Ulysses Grant became the leader of the Radicals.

RECONSTRUCTION ACTS

Two years after the Civil War the United Stated Congress passed four statutes, known as the Reconstruction Acts. The first was passed on March 2nd, 1867 to provide the more efficient Government of the Rebel states including Virginia, Texas, Florida, South Carolina, North Carolina, Mississippi, Alabama, Arkansas, Georgia, and Louisiana. The second, third, and fourth were passed to supplement the first act and to facilitate Restoration.

New constitutions were written in the South under the terms of the Reconstruction Acts. By 1868 Arkansas, North Carolina, South Carolina, Louisiana, Alabama and Florida were readmitted to the Union, after ratifying the 14th amendment required by the Reconstruction Act. Virginia, Mississippi, Texas and Georgia were readmitted in 1870.

RECONSTRUCTION IN THE SOUTH

Southerners believed that Reconstruction politicians were corrupt. They also believed that Reconstruction itself was corrupt and argued that overthrowing Reconstruction would bring an end to corruption and oppression and help to establish a responsible government.

Reconstruction efforts that attempted to put the freed blacks into mainstream America was a remarkable step for that time. Although it was not entirely successful, it left an important legacy in American society, which exemplifies the equality and civil rights that are in order today.

SCALAWAGS AND CARPETBAGGERS

Carpetbaggers were Northerners who moved to the South with freedmen. The phrase was originally coined from the term carpet bags, which are inexpensive luggage. A scalawag is a person who was White from the South who joined the Republican Party in the ex-Confederate area during reconstruction. Two of the most prominent Scalawags were General James Longstreet and Joseph Brown.

IMPEACHMENT

After Congress enacted the Reconstruction Act, the South divided into five military districts and the authority of the Army commander was supreme. The first attempt to impeach Johnson from office failed in 1867, when the House put together a bill of impeachment, which was basically a collection of complaints. In December of that year a formal vote was out in place with a 108-57 vote margin.

The House finally impeached Andrew Johnson in 1868 after he continued to oppose congressional policies and continued to insist on the removal of the radical secretary of War, Edwin M. Stanton. Although the radicals fell one vote short of convicting him, by this time Johnson's program had been effectively tarnished.

Civil Rights in the Aftermath of the War

FOURTEENTH AND FIFTEENTH AMENDMENTS

Three new constitutional amendments were adopted upon the end of the Civil War, the thirteenth abolished slavery and the fourteenth and fifteenth focused on the civil rights of slaves.

The fourteenth amendment to the United States constitution includes the Due Process and Equal Protection clauses among others. The fourteenth amendment requires that states provide protection under the law to all persons, granting all natural born or naturalized citizens federal and civil rights. The fourteenth amendment was exemplified during it interpretation to prohibit segregation in public schools and other facilities in Brown vs. Board of Education.

The fourteenth amendment was ratified in the following order:

Connecticut (June 25, 1866)

New Hampshire (July 6, 1866)

Tennessee (July 19, 1866)

New Jersey (September 11, 1866) - February 20, 1868 attempted to withdraw

Oregon (September 19, 1866)

Vermont (October 30, 1866)

Ohio (January 4, 1867) - January 15, 1868 attempted to withdraw

New York (January 10, 1867)

Kansas (January 11, 1867)

Illinois (January 15, 1867)

West Virginia (January 16, 1867)

Michigan (January 16, 1867)

Minnesota (January 16, 1867)

Maine (January 19, 1867)

Nevada (January 22, 1867)

Indiana (January 23, 1867)

Missouri (January 25, 1867)

Rhode Island (February 7, 1867)

Wisconsin (February 7, 1867)

Pennsylvania (February 12, 1867)

Massachusetts (March 20, 1867)

Nebraska (June 15, 1867)

Iowa (March 16, 1868)

Arkansas (April 6, 1868)

Florida (June 9, 1868)

North Carolina (July 4, 1868, after rejecting it on December 14, 1866)

Louisiana (July 9, 1868, after rejecting it on February 6, 1867)

South Carolina (July 9, 1868, after rejecting it on December 20, 1866)

Alabama (July 13, 1868, when the ratification was "approved" by the governor)

Georgia (July 21, 1868, after rejecting it on November 9, 1866)

The fifteenth amendment states that the governments of the United States of America may not prevent a person from voting because of their race, color, or previous condition of servitude.

FREEDMEN'S BUREAU

The Freedom's Bureau, also known as Bureau of Refugees or Freedmen and Abandoned Lands, became an agency to help freed slaves in the South, with shelter, housing and other essentials. It was established in 1865 by the United States Congress. It operated from June of 1865 through December 1868, until it was disbanded in 1872 because of funding issues.

CIVIL RIGHTS ACT

In March 1866, the first of several pieces of legislature was indicted in the United States that gave rights to the freed slaves after the Civil War. It was put together as a counterattack against the Black Codes in the South. Within the Civil Rights act 1866 was the right for persons of color to own private property, to have the ability to sue, to make contracts and be a witness in court.

President Andrew Johnson attempted to veto the bill arguing that it would give favor to the blacks over the whites. Yet, the republicans overrode the President's veto on April 9th and declared that all persons born in the United States were citizens, no matter what race, color, or previous condition. Those persons who denied the rights would be guilty of a misdemeanor and was punishable with a fine of up to $1,000 and/or imprisonment.

ELECTED BLACK OFFICE-HOLDERS

The Republicans took full control of Southern state governments and legislatures, this lead to the election of numerous African-American to state national offices, as well as other positions of power, nearly 137 black office holders lived outside the South, before the Civil War.

RESPONSE TO JOHNSON'S POLICIES

Reconstruction aroused intense opposition, slaveholders and non-slaveholders in the South were bitter over the loss of the war, as slaveholders were upset over losing their slaves. They lashed out at the reconstruction and denounced Republicans as traitors to their race. The economic hardships caused by the war influenced their hostilities to the high rise in taxation to aid in reconstruction programs.

RESTORATION OF WHITE GOVERNMENT

Reconstruction opponents called for white racial unity and believed scalawags to be traitors to their race and region and called for these scalawags to come home to the "white man's party." Within those states with white majorities convinced most whites to vote Democrat, this was enough to defeat the Reconstruction, which Southerners called redemption.

 End of Reconstruction

Florida, South Caroline and Louisiana continued to be dominated by Republicans. While the democratic President Rutherford B. Hayes promised things would get better in the South, but the formation of the "Solid South" had already begun as support for Hayes's democratic opponent, Samuel J. Tilden was favored.

The end of reconstruction was complete once all federal troops were withdrawn from the South. Yet while white rule was restored black people were deprived of many civil and political rights and the economics of their state remained depressed.

Sample Test Questions

1) What was the major cause that lead directly into the Civil War?

    A) The eleven Southern slave states declared their secession and intent for the expansion of slavery
    B) The election of Abraham Lincoln
    C) The political differences between the North and the South
    D) The formation of the Confederate States of America

The correct answer is A:) The eleven Southern slave states declared their secession and intent for the expansion of slavery. Although there were many issues that helped to initiate the Civil War, the main issue that caused the Civil War was the eleven Southern Slave states declaring their secession and intent for the expansion of slavery.

2) Which political party was essentially dissipated during the 1850's?

    A) Democratic Republicans
    B) Federalists
    C) Whigs
    D) Populists

The correct answer is C:) Whigs. The party was unable to come to a consensus on the issue of slavery and ultimately many of the members joined other parties.

3) The primary economical crop for the Southern states was cotton, what was the second largest crop produced in the South?

    A) Rice
    B) Tobacco
    C) Food crops
    D) Wheat

The correct answer is A:) Rice. Cotton was the primary crop for the Southern states, the next largest was rice, followed by tobacco.

4)   Why did prisoner exchange programs break down during the Civil War?

   A) The Union forces were gathering more prisoners than the South, and the South had none to trade.
   B) When the Union began using freed or runaway slaves as soldiers it created tension and the South wouldn't exchange them.
   C) The Southern forces were gathering so many more prisoners than the Union that the Union had none to trade.
   D) President Lincoln considered the practice unethical and discontinued exchanges.

The correct answer is B:) When the Union began using freed or runaway slaves as soldiers it created tension and the South wouldn't exchange them. The South was angered by the large numbers of former slaves who were enlisted and preferred to execute or enslave them.

5)   What was the primary reason for the formation of the Confederate States?

   A) To back the prospect and idealism of expanding the slave states
   B) To offer legal and government assistance to the states in secession
   C) To offer a government that stands behind slavery
   D) The election of Abraham Lincoln

The correct answer is A:) To back the prospect and idealism of expanding the slave states. The Confederate states felt no need to be a part of the United States government and did not agree with their moral, political, or economical view and to back the prospect and idealism of keeping and expanding slavery throughout the South, Southerners created their own government.

6)   What is known as the single bloodiest day of the war?

   A) Battle of Gettysburg
   B) Battle of Chancellorsville
   C) Battle of Antietam
   D) Battle of Shiloh

The correct answer is C:) The Battle of Antietam. It was the first battle to take place on Northern soil and there were over 20,000 casualties.

7) What country did the majority of the immigrants that settled in the United States come from during the early 1800's?

   A) Mexico
   B) Europe
   C) Ireland
   D) France

The correct answer is C:) Ireland. Due to the potato famine in Ireland the majority of immigrants were of Irish decent.

8) What was the most historically important act of the 20th Maine regiment?

   A) They relieved McClellan's forces at Antietam and were instrumental in Union victory.
   B) They held their position at Little Round Top and were essential to Union victory at Gettysburg.
   C) They aided General Sherman in his March to the Sea.
   D) The fact that they were the first all black regiment.

The correct answer is B:) They held their position at Little Round Top and were essential to the Union victory at Gettysburg. When they ran out of ammunition, the regiment charged with bayonets. If they hadn't held their position, the Battle of Gettysburg would most likely have been a Confederate victory.

9) What was the name of the group formed in 1833 for the purpose of abolition movements?

   A) Republican Party
   B) The Freedman Bureau
   C) Know Nothing Party
   D) The American Anti-slavery Society

The correct answer is D:) The American Anti-slavery Society. The American Anti-slavery society was formed in 1833 condemning slavery as a racial discriminating practice and a moral sin.

10) Which of the following correctly describes the Trent Affair?

    A) Southern leaders attempted to leave the country and seek aid from France. Their ships were attacked and sunk.
    B) Northern leaders were discovered to be leaking battle plans to the South. They were discovered and tried for treason.
    C) When Southern leaders boarded a British ship, it was stopped and they were arrested. This angered the British because it violated freedom of the seas.
    D) None of the above.

The correct answer is C:) When Southern leaders boarded a British ship, it was stopped and they were arrested. This angered the British because it violated freedom of the seas. The British demanded an apology and the release of the leaders. Lincoln acquiesced.

11) What was one of the first methods of abolitionists?

    A) Print anti-slavery literature
    B) Put together conventions and lectures about anti-slavery
    C) Gather like-minded individuals together
    D) Arrange marches and anti-slavery demonstrations

The correct answer is C:) Gather like-minded individuals together. The first method of the abolitionists was to gather like-minded people together, other methods included publishing anti-slavery literature, holding lectures and organizing safety nets for freed slaves.

12) What development allowed rifles to be used as combat weapons during the Civil War?

    A) Minie balls
    B) Assembly line production of the rifles
    C) More accurate sites
    D) Both A and C

The correct answer is A:) Minie balls. The minie ball allowed for quick loading without sacrificing accuracy.

13) What year was *Uncle Tom's Cabin* published?

    A) 1863
    B) 1849
    C) 1852
    D) 1865

The correct answer is C:) 1852. *Uncle Tom's Cabin* was published in 1852 with 300,000 copies being sold in the first year and was the bestselling novel of the 19th century.

14) Which Civil War battle was considered "Lee's masterpiece"?

    A) Chancellorsville
    B) Gettysburg
    C) Antietam
    D) Shiloh

The correct answer is A:) Chancellorsville. In a risky move, Lee sent a large portion of his army to march around the Union and surprise them.

15) What was the major effect of *Uncle Tom's Cabin* on society?

    A) It produced sympathy and understanding to the horrible treatment of slaves.
    B) It was said to have been the main source for abolition movements and was thought to have laid the groundwork for the American Civil War.
    C) It reached out to Northerners who eventually became members of Anti-slavery movements.
    D) Made Southern Slaveholders act in a kinder manner to their slaves.

The correct answer is B:) It was said to have been the main source for abolition movements and was thought to have laid the groundwork for the American Civil War. The impact of *Uncle Tom's Cabin* was so strong many believe that the novel laid the groundwork for the American Civil War, so much so that when the author met with Abraham Lincoln he was said to have commented, "So, this is the little lady who made this big war."

16) What was unique about Lincoln's election in 1860?

    A) He received a unanimous vote from all states.
    B) Not a single Southern state voted for him.
    C) He was the first Republican candidate.
    D) Both B and C.

The correct answer is B:) Not a single Southern state voted for him. This was the reason that many Southern state's initially seceded.

17) What was the reason behind the Mexican War?

    A) Mexico abolished slavery and demanded that the United States to do the same.
    B) When Mexico established its borders Texas established their borders further south, giving Texas more Mexican territory.
    C) General Santa Anna and the Mexican government were bitter over the annexation of Texas.
    D) Mexico refused to recognize Texas' annexation and announced its intent on taking it back.

The correct answer is D:) Mexico refused to recognize Texas' annexation and announced its intent on taking it back. A military conflict began between the United States, who became an ally with Texas, and Mexico when Mexico refused to recognize Texas' annexation and announced its intent to take it back.

18) The person who promised to expand the United States west was?

    A) Abraham Lincoln
    B) Andrew Jackson
    C) William Allen
    D) William Lloyd Garrison

The correct answer is B:) Andrew Jackson. Andrew Jackson promised to expand the US, stating that Americans had the right and it was their duty to extend its civilization.

19) Under what provision did California become a state?

    A) It agreed to pay a large sum of money.
    B) Its citizens had to apply for citizenship individually.
    C) It agreed to fight for the Union in the civil war.
    D) It was admitted as a free state.

The correct answer is D:) It was admitted as a free state. This was problematic because the Missouri Compromise Line would have split the state in half.

20) What was the promise made to the Indians who were forced to leave their lands?

    A) The federal government would never again take control of Indian reservations in the future
    B) $9,000,000 for their lands
    C) They would enact constitutional rights for all Indian descendants
    D) They could have all the land they wanted in the West

The correct answer is B:) $9,000,000 for their lands. The majority of the land Andrew Jackson seized was from the Indians, forcing five different Indian tribes from their homes and pushed them west. While some Indians retaliated with violence other pursued the journey with a promise, from Andrew Jackson, to purchase their lands from them for $9,000.000.

21) Who would have become president if both Lincoln and Johnson had been assassinated?

    A) Schuyler Colfax
    B) William H Seward
    C) Salmon P Chase
    D) General Grant

The correct answer is A:) Schuyler Colfax. Colfax was the current Speaker of the House.

22) Which major senator was involved in the Compromise of 1850?

    A) Senator Henry Clay
    B) Senator Joseph Underwood
    C) Senator Stephen Douglas
    D) Senator John Bell

The correct answer is A:) Senator Henry Clay.

23) What lead to the Missouri compromise?

    A) Missouri sought admission into the Union with a constitution to permit slavery.
    B) Missouri would not abide by the emancipation proclamation.
    C) Missouri cut off from mail circulation that included anti-slavery literature.
    D) Missouri declared its independence as a country of its own.

The correct answer is A:) Missouri sought admission into the Union with a constitution to permit slavery. In 1818 Missouri required admission to the Union with a constitution to allow slavery. Northerners feared that other states would assume this was a standard for admission, creating an unbalanced America.

24) Although many Confederate officials remained in the United States after the war, a large number also escaped to which country?

    A) Britain
    B) Nigeria
    C) Portugal
    D) Mexico

The correct answer is D:) Mexico.

25) What was the major crisis for the United States after the Mexican War?

    A) Congress was unsure what to do with the citizens that lived in Texas, California and New Mexico.
    B) Anti-slavery forces demanded that slavery be abolished from all lands surrounding Mexico.
    C) Congress was unsure whether to allow Texas as a slave-holding state.
    D) Texas sought to receive the benefits of the United States government, but did not want to be a part of the Union.

The correct answer is B:) Anti-slavery forces demanded that slavery be abolished from all lands surrounding Mexico. The major crisis for the United States after the Mexican war was the Anti-slavery forces that demanded that slavery to be abolished from all lands surrounding Mexico. Congress was so confused and divided over the anti-slavery and slavery groups no solution could be reached until the Compromise measures of 1850.

26) What was made McClellan an ineffective general?

    A) He was concerned about his political image and wanted to become president.
    B) He was overly cautious and wouldn't ever risk losing troops.
    C) His strategies tended to be too complex and ambitious so they ultimately failed.
    D) Both A and B.

The correct answer is D:) Both A and B. McClellan ran against Lincoln in the 1864 elections.

27) Kentucky was a slave state, but did not secede from the Union at the beginning of the war. Why did Kentucky later join the Union?

    A) Because of Confederates trying to win over the state.
    B) Because it was already the site of many major battles.
    C) Because the Union threatened to withdraw its soldiers protecting the area.
    D) Because they decided to they supported the abolition sentiment.

The correct answer is A:) Because of Confederates trying to win over the state.

28) Which Union general kept off the Confederate troops for the first day at Bull Run until more Union troops came?

    A) General Irvin McDowell
    B) General George McClellan
    C) General Thomas Jackson
    D) General Albert Johnston

The correct answer is A:) General Irvin McDowell.

29) What was the Compromise of 1850?

    A) The Compromise admitted California as a free state and set up governments in the remainder of the Mexican cession to decide whether to permit slavery there or not.

    B) Abolish slavery in New Mexico, California, Arizona and the Rocky Mountain States.

    C) To abolish slavery in New Mexico, California, but allow the Rocky Mountain States to determine whether or not they would like slavery for themselves.

    D) To admit California, New Mexico, Arizona and the Rocky Mountains as slave states.

The correct answer is A:) The Compromise admitted California as a free state and set up governments in the remainder of the Mexican cession to decide whether to permit slavery there or not. In January of 1850, Henry Clay introduced a series of compromises into Congress that would ultimately admit California as a free state and set up territorial governments in the remainder of the Mexican cession to decide for themselves whether to permit slavery or not. After seven months of various changes the compromise was passed in August of 1850.

30) What was surprising about the Second Battle of Bull Run?

    A) The South lost even though they had nearly double the troops the Union did.

    B) The Union lost even though they had nearly double the troops the South did.

    C) The Union had gotten a hold of the battle plans for the South, but they didn't follow them at the battle, throwing their strategy off.

    D) None of the above

The correct answer is B:) The Union lost even though they had nearly double the troops the South did.

31) The Senator who initiated the Kansas-Nebraska Act was?

    A) Senator Stephen A. Douglas

    B) Senator Jefferson Davis

    C) Senator Benjamin Franklin Wade

    D) Senator Charles Francis Adams, Sr.

The correct answer is A:) Senator Stephen A. Douglas. The US Senator from Illinois, Senator Stephen A. Douglas introduced a bill to organize the territories of Kansas and Nebraska to be divided into two territories, Kansas to be a Southern state and Nebraska as a Northern state.

32) Who was the Union general at the Battle of Shiloh?

    A) General Burnside
    B) General Johnston
    C) General Grant
    D) General McClellan

The correct answer is C:) General Grant.

33) Who was the Confederate general at the Battle of Shiloh?

    A) General Burnside
    B) General Johnston
    C) General Grant
    D) General McClellan

The correct answer is B:) General Johnston.

34) Where did a majority of the Generals in the Civil War receive their training?

    A) United States Military Academy
    B) They had no formal training
    C) West Point
    D) None of the above

The correct answer is C:) West Point.

35) The Republican Party formation came after what big event?

    A) The Missouri Compromise
    B) The Compromise of 1850
    C) The Kansas-Nebraska Act
    D) The Mexican War

The correct answer is C:) The Kansas-Nebraska Act. After the Kansas-Nebraska act the formation of the Republican Party, the party's founder demanded the revoke of the Kansas-Nebraska act denouncing slavery as sheer evil and opposed it altogether.

36) Which of the following BEST describes Lee's general strategy?

    A) Ambitious
    B) Defensive
    C) Offensive
    D) None of the above

The correct answer is B:) Defensive. Lee tended to have a defensive strategy. A notable exception from this strategy, however is the Battle of Gettysburg.

37) The main objective to John Brown's raid on Harper's Ferry was?

    A) To ambush soldiers that were camped out at Harper's Ferry.
    B) To halt all crossings to Harper's Ferry from the B&O railroad.
    C) To capture United States arsenal's that were stored on Harper's Ferry.
    D) To capture the town and stop all supplies from coming into the city.

The correct answer is C:) To capture United States arsenal's that were stored on Harper's Ferry. In October 1859 John Brown set out to journey across the Potomac River from Maryland to Virginia his main objective was to capture US arsenals that were stored on Harper's Ferry.

38) Which of the following was NOT an argument used by the South in defense of slavery?

    A) The large numbers of relatively free labor were essential to the Southern economy.
    B) Many biblical prophets had slaves, including Abraham.
    C) The Courts had supported the legality of slavery, as with Dred v. Scott.
    D) All of the above were used as arguments in defense of slavery.

The correct answer is D:) All of the above were used as arguments in defense of slavery. The South turned to everything from history to economics to politics to defend the practice of slavery.

39) What was the main issue that split the Democratic Party?

A) Issues of Slavery
B) The Republican Party
C) The Civil War
D) The Presidential election

The correct answer is A:) Issues of Slavery. Although 50 Southern democrats walked out over partisan issues, while the party was completely split over the issues of slavery.

40) Who was the Republican nominee in the 1856 election?

A) Abraham Lincoln
B) John C Fremont
C) James Buchanan
D) Stephen A Douglass

The correct answer is B:) John C Fremont. Fremont was the first candidate to run under the Republican Party.

41) Which was the first state to secede from the Union?

A) Mississippi
B) Alabama
C) Georgia
D) South Carolina

The correct answer is D:) South Carolina. South Carolina was the first state that made its secession from the United States; it had longed to secede and unite with Southern slave states.

42) Which of the following was NOT one of the original seven states to secede?

A) South Carolina
B) Georgia
C) Georgia
D) Missouri

The correct answer is D:) Missouri. The seven original states that seceded were South Carolina, Mississippi, Georgia, Florida, Louisiana, Alabama and Texas.

43) What are considered as the five Border States?

    A) West Virginia, Maryland, Delaware, Kentucky, and Missouri
    B) Kentucky, Tennessee, South Carolina, Missouri and Florida
    C) Florida, Georgia, Kentucky, Alabama, and South Carolina
    D) Georgia, Louisiana, Florida, Alabama, and South Carolina

The correct answer A:) West Virginia, Maryland, Delaware, Kentucky, and Missouri. The five Border States refer to the states that were on the border between the Northern Union States and the Southern Confederate States who were subdivided on the political, social, economic and geographical issues. Those states included West Virginia, Maryland, Delaware, Kentucky, and Missouri.

44) At the start of the Civil War there were two waves in which states seceded. What was each caused by?

    A) The first was caused by the election of Abraham Lincoln, and the second was caused when Lincoln sent troops to recover Fort Sumter.
    B) The first was caused by the raid at Harpers Ferry, and the second was caused by the election of Abraham Lincoln.
    C) The first was caused by the election of Abraham Lincoln, and the second was caused by the raid at Harpers Ferry.
    D) The first was caused by when Lincoln sent troops to recover Fort Sumter and the second occurred after the South won a major victory at the First Battle of Bull Run.

The correct answer is A:) The first was caused by the election of Abraham Lincoln and the second was caused when Lincoln sent troops to recover Fort Sumter.

45) Who was the President of the Confederate States of America?

    A) Robert E. Lee
    B) Jefferson Davis
    C) Braxton Bragg
    D) Nathan Bedford Forest

The correct answer is B:) Jefferson Davis. The President of the Confederate States was Jefferson Davis.

46) What do the Constitutions of the United States and Confederate States of America say about the right of secession?

    A) The United States Constitution does not allow it, but the Confederate States Constitution did.
    B) The Confederate States Constitution did not allow it, but the United States Constitution does.
    C) Both the United States and the Confederate States Constitutions declare it illegal.
    D) Neither of the Constitutions even mentions the right of secession.

The correct answer is D:) Neither of the Constitutions even mentions the right of secession. The Confederate Constitution was essentially an altered copy of the United States Constitution, however it did not address the matter of secession.

47) Which state was President Lincoln referring to when he said, "I think to lose _____ is nearly the same as to lose the whole game"?

    A) Maryland
    B) Virginia
    C) Kentucky
    D) Tennessee

The correct answer is C:) Kentucky.

48) How many armies in the Confederate states were there altogether?

    A) 6
    B) 12
    C) 11
    D) 15

The correct answer is B:) 12. There were a total of 12 armies in the Confederate states including: Army of Peninsula, Forests Cavalry Corps, the Army of the Valley, Army of the West, the Army of the Northern Virginia, the Army of the Northwest, the Army of New Mexico, Army of Kanawha, Army of Tennessee, Army of Kentucky, the Army of Middle Tennessee, and the Army of Mississippi.

49) Which of the following BEST describes the difference between War Democrats and Peace Democrats during the Civil War?

    A) War Democrats and Peace Democrats both considered Lincoln a good president. However, Peace Democrats did not support the war against the Confederacy.
    B) War Democrats supported Lincoln as president and the war whereas Peace Democrats did not support either.
    C) War Democrats and Peace Democrats both disagreed with the Republican policies. However, War Democrats did agree with fighting the Confederacy.
    D) None of the above

The correct answer is C:) War Democrats and Peace Democrats both disagreed with the Republican policies. However, War Democrats did agree with fighting the Confederacy. Peace Democrats came to be known as Copperheads.

50) Who had more of an advantage when the war began the North or South?

    A) Although the North had a larger population, the South had more of an advantage due to only having to defend their lands as opposed to having to invade.
    B) The North had more men, a larger section of railroad and had the majority of factories that created war materials, which seemed to take an advantage over the South.
    C) The South had an advantage over the North because the North had draft rioters, bounty jumpers and Northerners grew tired of the war early on, making many of their eligible soldiers made to stay in the North to calm Northerners and enforce conscription.
    D) The North took advantage over the South with many Southerners profiteering (running luxury runs through the blockade rather than war supplies), evading taxes and draft dodging.

The correct answer is B:) The North had more men, a larger section of railroad and had the majority of factories that created war materials, which seemed to take an advantage over the South. The North's combined population was nearly 22 million people, combined with the number of soldiers enrolling to serve and having the majority of factories that produced war material, as well as the North having a good section of a railroad gave the North more advantages.

51) Which of the following best describes recruitment methods during the Civil War?

    A) Each side initially relied on volunteers, but were soon turned to drafting and conscription.
    B) Each side was able to rely throughout the war on volunteer armies.
    C) The South relied heavily on slaves and conscription while the North raised volunteers.
    D) The South turned to foreign armies for aid and the North relied heavily on drafting and recruitment of former slaves.

The correct answer is A:) Each side initially relied on volunteers but were soon turned to drafting and conscription. Although the problem came earlier for the South than the North, draft and conscription were key to recruitment in the Civil War.

52) How did the South finally earn the victory of the First Manassas (Bull Run)?

    A) General Thomas Jackson, also known as "Stonewall," he showed up with reinforcements for the Confederate army earning a victory over the North.
    B) General Thomas Jackson cut the lines of materials and supplies off to the armies.
    C) The North surrendered their armies.
    D) When the North went for reinforcements the South attacked the South.

The correct answer is A:) General Thomas Jackson, also known as "Stonewall," he showed up with reinforcements for the Confederate army earning a victory over the North. Although the battle did begin in the Northerners favor.

53) What was the last major Confederate victory in the West?

    A) Battle of Gettysburg
    B) Battle of Chickamauga
    C) Battle of Mobile
    D) Battle of Chancellorsville

The correct answer is B:) Battle of Chickamauga. The battle was a part of Sherman's Atlanta Campaign and was the first major battle to take place in Georgia.

54) What was the first state to be admitted back to the Union?

    A) Arkansas
    B) North Carolina
    C) Florida
    D) Tennessee

The correct answer is D:) Tennessee.

55) The fear Southerners had with Republican control was?

    A) The expansion of slavery would be stopped and the extinction of slavery would soon follow.
    B) Southerners feared with the Republican under control the Confederate Army would loss its grip on the Civil War and the Union would defeat them.
    C) They would take over the Senate and have the power to enforce laws and taxes.
    D) The South feared that with the Republican Party would do everything in their power to see the Civil War won by the Northerners.

The correct answer is A:) The expansion of slavery would be stopped and the extinction of slavery would soon follow. Southerners feared that the Republican Party, with the election of Abraham Lincoln the expansion of slavery would be stopped and the slavery would become extinct soon after.

56) What did the compromise of 1850 accomplish?

I. Set up territorial governments in the remainder of the Mexican cession to decide for themselves whether to permit slavery or not.
II. Admitted California as a free state.
III. Revoked the Missouri compromise and provided that settlers in the territories should decide for themselves "all questions pertaining to slavery."

    A) All three
    B) Both I and II
    C) Both II and III
    D) None of the above

The correct answer is B:) Both I and II.

57) Who was fired for their "inaction" before Sherman's march to Atlanta?

A) General Johnson
B) General Meade
C) General McClellan
D) General Burnside

The correct answer is A:) General Johnson. Lincoln had to go through a number of generals before finally finding one who wouldn't jeopardize their chance of winning by hesitating.

58) Although Congress and Lincoln's relationship varied, what were the main issues Lincoln presented that were passed into laws?

A) A homestead bill, land subsidies, an increase in the Tariff, and grants to promote agricultural growth.
B) Abolition, slavery and civil rights laws.
C) A homestead bill, civil rights of freed slaves, an increase in Tariff and grants that promote agricultural growth.
D) Land subsidies, an increase in Tariff, a homestead bill, and laws for freed slaves.

The correct answer is A:) A homestead bill, land subsidies, an increase in the Tariff, and grants to promote agricultural growth. Congress passed into law the following issues that were presented by Abraham Lincoln and his administration; A Homestead bill, land subsidies, an increase in Tariff and grants that promote agricultural growth.

59) How were women in the North and South fundamentally different before the war?

A) Northern women tended to be reformers, whereas Southern women were domestic and subservient.
B) Southern women tended to be reformers, whereas Northern women were domestic and subservient.
C) Northern women tended to be compassionate and charity motivated whereas Southern women were more concerned about political rights and issues.
D) None of the above

The correct answer is A:) Northern women tended to be reformers, whereas Southern women were domestic and subservient.

60) The basic meaning behind the Emancipation Proclamation was?

    A) The Emancipation Proclamation was a congressional order to free all the slave states in the United States of America.

    B) The Proclamation simply stated that all slaves in the Union states be free and have the same rights and privileges as all other citizens in the North.

    C) The Emancipation Proclamation was a Presidential order to free all slaves in the area of the Confederate States of America.

    D) The proclamation stated that all free slaves within the Union and Confederate states should be enacted into the United States as normal abiding citizens.

The correct answer is C:) The Emancipation Proclamation was a Presidential order to free all slaves in the area of the Confederate States of America.

61) What set Grant apart from other Union generals?

    A) He was disliked by many of the men because of his hesitance to attack.

    B) He was one of the only generals in the war who did not attend West Point which gave him an edge over the others.

    C) While many of them were concerned about their political appearance, he was concerned about and loved by his men.

    D) None of the above

The correct answer is C:) While many of them were concerned about their political appearance, he was concerned about and loved by his men.

62) When Conscription was passed what were the fears of those who opposed it?

    A) Soldiers who were forced into battle would make poor fighting men and it compromised volunteer soldiers from enlisting, seeing the conscription as an act of desperation.

    B) That conscription would cause riots and rioters who opposed the war and were not willing to fight for it.

    C) Those who opposed the conscription felt it was an invasion of individual interests and feared those who were forced to fight would give up easily and help their opponents win the battle, or surrender to end the war.

    D) Conscription would make volunteer soldiers to have low mortality rates; by the thought of the desperation of war hands their spirits would be broken.

The correct answer is A:) Soldiers who were forced into battle would make poor fighting men and it compromised volunteer soldiers from enlisting, seeing the conscription as an act of desperation.

63) Which of the following BEST describes the Emancipation Proclamation?

   A) It freed all slaves in North America
   B) It freed all slaves in the Union and Confederacy
   C) It freed all slaves in the Confederacy
   D) None of the above

The correct answer is C:) It freed all slaves in the Confederacy.

64) How many conscription acts were passed into law throughout the Civil War?

   A) One
   B) Four
   C) Three
   D) Two

The correct answer is C:) Three. Three were a total of three conscription acts that passed into law, on the 16th of April 1862, calling for men between the ages of 18-35, the age limit was raised in September of 1862 to include men up to the age of 45, and in February of 1864 the call of men went to all men between the ages of 17-50.

65) Which of the following is NOT true of the Compromise of 1850?

   A) It abolished slave trade in Washington DC.
   B) It allowed California to enter as a free state.
   C) It included the Fugitive Slave Act.
   D) It allowed Idaho to enter as a free state.

The correct answer is D:) It allowed Idaho to enter as a free state. The Compromise attempted to smooth over relations between the North and South, but it was just a temporary solution.

66) The Federal Government themselves stated they were fighting for what?

   A) To protect the Northern States
   B) To save the Union
   C) To free the Slaves
   D) To abolish the Confederacy

The correct answer is B:) To save the Union. The federal government admitted that they were actually fighting to save the Union.

67) Which of the following BEST describes the Confederate strategy in the Civil War?

    A) They wanted to outlast the Union so that they would have to concede.
    B) They wanted to force the Union off of Southern soil and launch an offensive.
    C) They wanted to lure the Union forces into remote areas and slowly destroy the army one battalion at a time.
    D) They wanted a political solution in which the Union agreed to formally recognize them as a sovereign country and discontinue fighting.

The correct answer is A:) They wanted to outlast the Union so that they would have to concede. The South knew that the Union had limited resources, was not on their own soil and started the war with a few bad defeats. They knew if they just held on long enough they would eventually win.

68) The South hoped for European aid, how did they feel they would be able to receive that?

    A) Europe would have never been involved with fighting for the preservation of slavery, therefore when the scope of the war changed in 1862 they attempted to convince Europe they could aid the South without aiding slavery.
    B) The South asked for the aid of Europe in exchange for cotton, Europe was the biggest buyer of cotton before the Civil War began.
    C) The South offered Europe a partnership with the cotton plantations for their aid throughout the Civil War.
    D) Europe would have loved to see the democracy of the United States to be destroyed, proving a democracy doesn't work. Therefore the South was hoping for the Monarchy to step up to democracy.

The correct answer is A:) Europe would have never been involved with fighting for the preservation of slavery, therefore when the scope of the war changed in 1862 they attempted to convince Europe they could aid the South without aiding slavery.

69) Who was in charge of the prisoner of war camp Andersonville?

    A) Captain Henry Wirz
    B) Judah P Benjamin
    C) Salmon P Chase
    D) Edwin M Stanton

The correct answer is A:) Captain Henry Wirz. After the war, he was tried and executed for war crimes.

70) After the Battle of Fredericksburg and being disappointed once again, what did Lincoln do?

   A) He called for the Surrender of Confederate Troops
   B) Lincoln relieved Ambrose Burnside as Commander of the Army of the Potomac and appointed Joseph Hooker
   C) He called for the surrender of Union Troops
   D) He planned, himself, a major attack on the Confederate Army

The correct answer is B:) Lincoln relieved Ambrose Burnside as Commander of the Army of the Potomac and appointed Joseph Hooker.

71) Which state was originally neutral in the Civil War?

   A) Maryland
   B) Kentucky
   C) West Virginia
   D) Nebraska

The correct answer is B:) Kentucky. Kentucky was a border state and a hotbed of conflict. Although it was originally neutral, a failed attempt at takeover by the Confederacy caused it to seek alliance with the Union.

72) The Eastern Theatre consisted of what states?

   A) Mississippi, Pennsylvania, Alabama, Virginia, and the District of Columbia
   B) West Virginia, Virginia, Pennsylvania, New York and the District of Columbia
   C) Virginia, West Virginia, Maryland, Pennsylvania, and the District of Columbia
   D) New York, Maryland, Virginia, Pennsylvania, and Virginia

The correct answer is C:) Virginia, West Virginia, Maryland, Pennsylvania, and the District of Columbia.

73) Name the three theater operations.

   A) The Eastern Theater, the Western Theater, and the Trans-Mississippi Theater
   B) The Union, The confederacy and the Army of the Potomac
   C) The Western Theater, The Eastern Theater and the Naval Army
   D) The Eastern Theater, Western Theater, Northern Theater and Southern Theater

The correct answer is A:) The Eastern Theater, the Western Theater, and the Trans-Mississippi Theater.

74) A victory in which place helped Lincoln win the election of 1864?

   A) Gettysburg
   B) Shiloh
   C) Atlanta
   D) Antietam

The correct answer is C:) Atlanta. Northern support for the war was beginning to dwindle by this point and a publicized victory in Atlanta helped boost morale and favor of Lincoln.

75) What States did the Western Theater consist of?

   A) New England and North and South Carolina
   B) The Carolina's, Maine, New Jersey, and New York
   C) Georgia, the Carolinas, East of the Mississippi and West of the Appalachian Mountains
   D) California, New Mexico, Texas, and Illinois

The correct answer is C:) Georgia, the Carolinas, East of the Mississippi and West of the Appalachian Mountains.

76) What was Lee's strategy at Chancellorsville?

   A) To confront the army head on because he had a larger number of troops.
   B) To back the army into the river and force them to surrender.
   C) To sneak around them in the city at night and attack from all sides in the morning.
   D) To organize a surprise attack from the rear.

The correct answer is D:) To organize a surprise attack from the rear. He sent the majority of his army around the Union army and surprised them from behind. It was called Lee's masterpiece.

77) In the beginning of 1863, who seemed to be taking advantage of the war?

    A) The Union Military
    B) The Northern Theater
    C) The Western Theater
    D) The Confederate Military

The correct answer is D:) The Confederate Military.

78) Which state is Fort Sumter in?

    A) North Carolina
    B) Georgia
    C) Virginia
    D) South Carolina

The correct answer is D:) South Carolina.

79) How were relations between the Radical Republicans in Congress and Johnson during Reconstruction?

    A) Their opinions were almost always in line.
    B) They had a reasonable amount of disagreement, however they were still able to work together.
    C) They were in opposition on many issues and eventually impeached him.
    D) None of the above

The correct answer is C:) They were in opposition on many issues and eventually impeached him. They purposely passed the Tenure of Office Act knowing that he would violate it and they would have grounds for impeachment.

80) Why were the Peace Democrats organized?

    A) To put an end to the Civil War.
    B) To abolish slavery altogether.
    C) To listen to what the people of the states were saying and educate others about the moral wrong doings of slaveholders.
    D) Huge casualty lists, rights violations, the emancipation, wartime failures, and the draft.

The correct answer is D:) Huge casualty lists, rights violations, the emancipation, wartime failures, and the draft.

81) The terms of Lee's surrender to Grant were

    A) Lenient. He allowed them all to return home and even keep their guns and horses.
    B) Harsh. He took prisoner all of the major generals and confiscated all weapons and ammunition.
    C) Lenient. He confiscated all weapons and ammunition but allowed everyone to return home.
    D) None of the above

The correct answer is A:) Lenient. He allowed them all to return home and even keep their guns and horses.

82) Throughout the first half of the war, during 1863, how many casualties had already suffered?

    A) 100,000 Union soldiers were casualties, the Confederate counted 93,000 soldiers killed.
    B) 260,000 Union soldiers were casualties, the Confederate counted 93,000 soldiers killed.
    C) 360,000 Union soldiers were casualties, the Confederate counted 193,000 soldiers killed.
    D) 360,000 Union soldiers were casualties, the Confederate counted 93,000 soldiers killed.

The correct answer is D:) 360,000 Union soldiers were casualties, the Confederate counted 93,000 soldiers killed.

83) Which of the following does the 14th Amendment NOT do?

    A) Define citizenship
    B) Gave all male citizens the right to vote
    C) Denied previous Confederate leaders the right to run for office
    D) Agree that the government will pay compensation for freed slaves

The correct answer is D:) Agree that the government will pay compensation for freed slaves. The amendment stated that compensation would NOT be paid.

84) What was the major cause of death to soldiers serving in the Civil War?

    A) Attacks from opposing armies
    B) Friendly fire
    C) Disease such as Typhoid fever diarrhea, and dysentery
    D) In the Civil War prison camps

The correct answer is C:) Disease such as Typhoid fever diarrhea, and dysentery. The leading cause of death to Civil War soldiers was diseases such as Typhoid fever diarrhea, and dysentery. About 620,000 soldiers died in the Civil War (on both sides).

85) How were captured soldiers, prisoners of war, handled at the beginning of war?

    A) War prisoners were exchanged on the battlefield
    B) They were sent back to their home states
    C) Kept in prison camps
    D) Killed by assassination

The correct answer is A:) War prisoners were exchanged on the battlefield. At the beginning of the war prisoners were exchanged on the battlefield, until the Secretary of war, Edwin M. Staton, stopped the exchange of prisoners on the battlefield. Prisoners were then kept in prison camps.

86) How did the Confederacy fund the Civil War?

    A) Borrowing
    B) Taxes
    C) Pirating European ships
    D) None of the above

The correct answer is B:) Taxes. Both the Union and Confederacy taxed and sold bonds to raise money for the war.

87) The role of women in the war was?

    A) Woman served to keep the spirits up for the soldiers throughout the Civil War
    B) They cooked for the soldiers at their base
    C) Woman served as housekeepers in the Civil War camps
    D) Woman served as volunteer nurses in the war

The correct answer is D:) Woman served as volunteer nurses in the war. Although few women dressed as men and fought in the war alongside their spouses, brothers and sons.

88) How did Johnson's "swing around the circle" tour effect opinion of him?

   A) It was disastrous and most likely lost him many Northern votes.
   B) It was highly successful and was the reason that he was able to run a second term.
   C) It had very little impact on his campaign either positive or negative.
   D) None of the above

The correct answer is A:) It was disastrous and most likely lost him many Northern votes. In the speaking tour, Johnson specifically attacked many of his Republican opponents and created a bad image for himself.

89) The name of the first official black infantry was called?

   A) Freedman's Theater
   B) The 54th Massachusetts Volunteer Infantry
   C) The Army of Northerners
   D) The 1st regiment to the Union

The correct answer is B:) The 54th Massachusetts Volunteer Infantry.

90) How did the rifles used during the Civil War effect the wounds?

   A) They made wide openings that left many permanently disabled.
   B) They made clean entries that killed quickly.
   C) They caused bones to shatter.
   D) None of the above

The correct answer is C:) They caused bones to shatter. The rifles hadn't been used in war before because they were difficult to load.

91) The first state to allow freed slaves to enlist in the army was?

   A) Tennessee
   B) Louisiana
   C) Ohio
   D) New York

The correct answer is A:) Tennessee. Tennessee was the first state to allow freed slaves to enlist and serve in the war.

92) Why was Picket reluctant to make his charge at Gettysburg?

    A) He felt that it was a lost cause.
    B) He considered himself inadequate.
    C) He thought that a sneak attack would be a better strategy.
    D) None of the above

The correct answer is B:) He considered himself inadequate. All of Pickett's men were either captured or killed as a result of the charge.

93) What event prompted the secessionists to attack Fort Sumter?

    A) Lincoln announced plans to re-supply the fort
    B) Fort Sumter threatened to attack
    C) They became impatient with the siege
    D) General McDowell arrived with troops

The correct answer is A:) Lincoln announced plans to re-supply the fort.

94) What were the most important victories for the Union in 1863?

    A) Gettysburg and Vicksburg
    B) Vicksburg and Chickamauga
    C) Chickamauga and Chancellorsville
    D) Chancellorsville and Murfreesboro

The correct answer is A:) Gettysburg and Vicksburg.

95) Which of the following BEST describes how did Wendell Phillips felt about the Emancipation Proclamation?

    A) He was an ardent abolitionist and supported the action as a move toward equality.
    B) He was highly opposed to abolition and resented the move.
    C) He was initially opposed to it, but agreed that it was the only way to end the war.
    D) None of the above

The correct answer is A:) He was an ardent abolitionist and supported the action as a move toward equality. Throughout the war, Phillips was highly critical of Lincoln's administration as he felt that the South should just be left alone to practice slavery, which he was opposed to.

96) Copperheads were?

A) Union Soldiers who left their posts.
B) Republicans who became democrats through the war.
C) Northerners who opposed Lincoln and his administration.
D) Peace Democrats from the North who opposed the Civil War and Lincoln and his administration.

The correct answer is D:) Peace Democrats from the North who opposed the Civil War and Lincoln and his administration.

97) Who was targeted during the New York Draft Riots?

I. Government officials
II. Families not drafted
III. Blacks

A) I only
B) III only
C) I and II only
D) I and III only

The correct answer is D:) I and III only. While the rioters initially attacked government buildings and officials who got in the way, they quickly turned to attacking blacks, both on the streets and in places such as orphanages.

98) What made the Chickamauga Battle so significant to the Union?

A) It made the Union realize they had stronger troops, better artillery and kept their hopes up for a quick surrender from the Confederacy.
B) It was the only war that Union troops can say they won without a real fight or loss of men.
C) It marked the end of the Union offense in Central Tennessee and Northwestern Georgia.
D) After the war the Confederates declared the war would be won by the Union and called back its troops.

The correct answer is C:) It marked the end of the Union offense in Central Tennessee and Northwestern Georgia.

99) Which of the following statements correctly describes the Twenty Slave Law of Virginia?

A) A person could not own more than twenty slaves without paying increased income taxes.
B) A person could not own more than twenty slaves under any circumstances.
C) A person who owned more than twenty slaves was exempted from drafting.
D) A person could pay the equivalent of the value of twenty slaves to be exempted from drafting.

The correct answer is C:) A person who owned more than twenty slaves was exempted from drafting. This created anger because it essentially allowed the "rich" to get out of fighting.

100) The names of the three battles of Chattanooga were?

A) The Battle of the Chattanooga, the Battle of Lookout Mountain and the Battle of the Union Barricades
B) The Battle of Chattanooga, the Battle of Lookout Mountain and the Battle of the Missionary Ridge
C) The Battle of Tennessee, the Battle of Lookout Mountains and the Battle of Chattanooga
D) The Battle of the Tall Mountains, the Battle of Chattanooga and the Battle of the Missionary Ridge

The correct answer is B:) The Battle of Chattanooga, the Battle of Lookout Mountain and the Battle of the Missionary Ridge. The three battles that were fought during the time of the Chattanooga were The Battle of Chattanooga, the Battle of Lookout Mountain and the Battle of the Missionary Ridge.

101) How did Lincoln feel about letting blacks serve in the Union army?

A) He was opposed to it, worrying that it would incite the South even more.
B) He was opposed to it because he didn't believe that they were equal to whites.
C) He was in favor of it and just needed to wait for the war to shift in favor of the Union to announce it as legal. This way he increased the chance that the people would support it.
D) He was reluctant, though his opinion eventually shifted and the Emancipation Proclamation gave them the right.

The correct answer is D:) He was reluctant, though his opinion eventually shifted and the Emancipation Proclamation gave them the right. Throughout the war, Lincoln held his claim that the war was not about freeing slaves, but preserving the Union. All of his moves reflected this.

102) Gettysburg was said to be one of the bloodiest battled of the American Civil War, how many casualties were there in the Gettysburg alone?

A) 65,000
B) 75,000
C) 59,000
D) 51,000

The correct answer is D:) 51,000.

103) Why is Lee's victory of the Peninsula Campaign considered ironic?

A) Because he had intended to lose and trick the North into thinking they were weak.
B) Because he had so many fewer troops than the North than no one thought he would win.
C) Because in this case, victory meant that the war would be prolonged and continued fighting.
D) None of the above

The correct answer is C:) Because in this case, victory meant that the war would be prolonged and continued fighting.

104) The Savannah Campaign was commonly known as?

A) The Siege of Petersburg
B) Sherman's March to the Sea
C) The Fall of Richmond
D) Sherman's Atlanta Campaign

The correct answer is B:) Sherman's March to the Sea. The Savanna Campaign was commonly known as Sherman's March to the Sea.

105) Why was Johnson impeached?

A) Because his actions towards Native Americans were violations of Bill of Rights freedoms.
B) Because it was discovered that he had illegally gathered campaign funds.
C) Because by firing his Secretary of War he violated the Tenure of Office Act.
D) None of the above

The correct answer is C:) Because by firing his Secretary of War he violated the Tenure of Office Act.

106) General Albert Johnston raised what army to defend Confederate lines?

A) The Army of Tennessee
B) The Army of Texas
C) The Army of the Mississippi
D) The Army of the Ohio River

The correct answer is C:) The Army of the Mississippi. General Albert Johnston raised The Army of the Mississippi.

107) What is considered the start of the Civil War?

A) Battle of Fort Sumter
B) First Battle of Bull Run
C) The secession of South Carolina
D) None of the above

The correct answer is A:) Battle of Fort Sumter. After Lincoln sent troops to Fort Sumter, the second wave of states seceded from the Union. Because it is the first place fighting occurred, it is considered the start of the war.

108) General Forest was a Confederate Army General and instrumental figure in founding what group?

A) The Ku Klux Klan
B) The Anti-slavery association
C) The Peace Democrats
D) The In the Know Party

The correct answer is A:) The Ku Klux Klan. Forest was one of the founding fathers of the Ku Klux Klan.

109) When did the Shenandoah Valley cease to be strategically important for the Confederacy?

A) When Petersburg became more important
B) After General Sheridan's Valley Campaign
C) When General Early was relieved of command
D) When Sherman's March destroyed the area

The correct answer is B:) After General Sheridan's Valley Campaign.

110) Why did McClellan lose the 1864 election?

I. He didn't have the funds to properly campaign.
II. The war started going well and Lincoln returned to favor.
III. His peace platform was too idealistic.

    A) II only
    B) III only
    C) II and III only
    D) I and II only

The correct answer is C:) II and III only.

111) In the Battle of the Atlanta what was Sherman's plan to defeat the Confederates?

    A) To burn the town to the ground
    B) Cut off and destroy supply troops
    C) To strike from behind without the Confederates ever knowing, to take them by surprise
    D) Hold the city hostage until the Confederates surrendered

The correct answer is B:) Cut off and destroy supply troops.

112) Which of the following correctly lists the four slave states that did NOT secede during the Civil War?

    A) Delaware, Kentucky, Maryland, Missouri
    B) Missouri, Kentucky, Texas, Georgia
    C) Texas, Maryland, Delaware, Missouri
    D) Kentucky, Texas, Delaware, Maryland

The correct answer is A:) Delaware, Kentucky, Maryland, Missouri.

113) What was the effect of the Battle of Mobile Bay?

    A) The reelection of Abraham Lincoln
    B) The Navy's surrender
    C) The close on Mobile Bay
    D) The closer of two Confederate ports

The correct answer is A:) The reelection of Abraham Lincoln. The battle of Mobile greatly affected the re-election of Abraham Lincoln.

114) Who did the majority of abandoned southern plantations go to?

    A) Their former owners
    B) Their governing state
    C) The federal government
    D) They were destroyed

The correct answer is A:) Their former owners.

115) Which of the following best describes the result of the Northwestern Conspiracy?

    A) Because Copperheads opposed President Lincoln's policies, they accepted bribes to carry out a rebellion. They stole and destroyed a large store of weapons and supplies for the war.
    B) Because Copperheads were too afraid of the political consequences of rebellion, the conspiracy was never actually carried through.
    C) Because Copperheads allowed military plans to fall into the hands of Southern Generals, many more soldiers were lost than were necessary.
    D) None of the above

The correct answer is B:) Because Copperheads were too afraid of the political consequences of rebellion, the conspiracy was never actually carried through. Copperheads were Peace Democrats who did not support the war effort.

116) Who helped the Union win at Appomattox toward the end of the war?

    A) Major General Sherman
    B) Major General Sheridan
    C) Major General Custer
    D) Major General Gordon

The correct answer is C:) Major General Custer.

117) Grant created what army that would eventually change its name to the Army of the Northeastern Virginia?

    A) The Army of Virginia
    B) The Army of the Potomac
    C) The Army of Virginia
    D) The Army of the Cumberland

The correct answer is B:) The Army of the Potomac.

118) What were the four main battles that won Lee his fame throughout the Civil War?

A) The Seven Days Battle, the Battle of Chancellorsville, Gettysburg and Mobile
B) The Seven Days Battle, the Battle of Chancellorsville, the Battle of the Fredericksburg, and the Second Battle of Bull Run
C) The Battle of the Fredericksburg, the First Manassas, the Fall of Richmond and the Second Battle of Bull Run
D) The Seven Days Battle, the Battle of Chancellorsville, the Atlanta Battle and the fall of Richmond

The correct answer is B:) The Seven Days Battle, the Battle of Chancellorsville, the Battle of the Fredericksburg, and the Second Battle of Bull Run. The four major battles that Lee served in and made him famous was the Seven Days Battle, the Battle of Chancellorsville, the Battle of the Fredericksburg, and the Second Battle of Bull Run.

119) Why was the North becoming dissatisfied with Lincoln?

A) The North grew dissatisfied with President Lincoln because the battle loses had been staggering and Grant hadn't taken Richmond or destroyed Lee's army.
B) The North grew dissatisfied with President Lincoln because the war wasn't over yet.
C) The North grew dissatisfied with President Lincoln because of inflation.
D) The North grew dissatisfied with President Lincoln because the armies were losing so many soldiers during battles.

The correct answer is A:) The North grew dissatisfied with President Lincoln, with the battle loses had been staggering and Grant hadn't taken Richmond or destroyed Lee's army.

120) Where did Lee finally surrender?

A) Appomattox
B) The Fall of Richmond
C) Fredericksburg
D) Overland Campaign

The correct answer is A:) Appomattox.

121) How were black soldiers treated?

A) Captured African-American soldiers were forced to fight on the front lines of the Confederate Army.
B) Captured African-American soldiers were not treated with equality by Confederate troops and were treated as runaway slaves. If their owners could not be located they were put to work to support the Confederate war effort.
C) Captured African-American soldiers were not treated with equality by Confederate troops and were treated as runaway slaves and placed in prisons.
D) Captured African-American soldiers were not treated with equality by Confederate troops and were sold to South slave-owners and the money was used for the Confederate army.

The correct answer is B:) Captured African-American soldiers were not treated with equality by Confederate troops and were treated as runaway slaves. If their owners could not be located they were put to work to support the Confederate war effort.

122) Who was Clara Barton?

A) Clara Barton was a driving force for the Union army when she dressed up like a man and fought in the front lines.
B) Clara Barton was a major player in the care for wounded soldiers and she helped to create the American branch of the International Red Cross.
C) Clara Barton was the Leader of the Army base hospitals.
D) Clara Barton led the revolution which ended the Civil War.

The correct answer is B:) Clara Barton was a major player in the care for wounded soldiers and she helped to create the American branch of the International Red Cross. She also became a major participant in the creation of the American branch of the International Red Cross.

123) The Battle of the Wilderness was the first battle Ulysses S. Grant fourth in 1864, for how many days did the battle last?

A) Two
B) One
C) Three
D) Seven

The correct answer is A:) Two.

124) The Battle of the Cold Harbor is remembered as what?

    A) America's bloodiest campaign
    B) The worse attack on Confederate troops
    C) The biggest loss of life in American history
    D) The coldest battle in the Civil War

The correct answer is A:) America's bloodiest campaign.

125) Grant sent the army of _____, commanded by _____ to defeat the forces of Jubal Anderson Early at the Shenandoah Valley, what was the name of the army and the commander?

    A) The Potomac, Phillip Sheradon
    B) The Tennessee, Oliver O. Howards
    C) The Ohio, Schofield
    D) The Shenandoah, David Hunter

The correct answer is A:) The Potomac, Phillip Sheradon.

126) The siege of Petersburg was also known as?

    A) The Battle of Petersburg
    B) The stall of Petersburg
    C) The Petersburg Campaign
    D) Richmond-Petersburg Campaign

The correct answer is D:) The Richmond-Petersburg Campaign.

127) What type of war was the Siege of Petersburg?

    A) Months of guerilla warfare
    B) A battle that was said to have grace
    C) Sneaky sudden attacks
    D) Ten months of trench warfare

The correct answer is D:) Ten months of trench warfare.

128) What were states' rights?

A) Each state possess certain rights and political powers in relation to the Federal government.
B) Each state having the ability to put into action what they feel would work best for their states political background and future plans.
C) The right to be a citizen in the state of choice for those after the war and the states right to not allow you to live in their state without prior approval.
D) The right to be a slave state or a non-slave state was up to each state.

The correct answer is A:) Each state possess certain rights and political powers in relation to the federal government.

129) Each General had a personal strategy for attack or defense, what was Colonel Sherman's strategy?

A) Sherman's strategy was to crush the Confederacy's rebellions
B) Sherman's strategy was to crush the opponents economically, strategically and psychologically
C) His strategy was to attack quick and quiet
D) Wait for the opposing Army to be spotted

The correct answer is B:) Sherman's strategy was to crush the opponents economically, strategically and psychologically.

130) What was the first battle between generals Grant and Lee?

A) The Battle of Vicksburg
B) The Battle of Chancellorsville
C) The Battle of the Wilderness
D) The Battle of Gettysburg

The correct answer is C:) Battle of the Wilderness.

131) How many soldiers lost their lives during the Siege of Petersburg, combining both Union and Confederate?

A) 28,000 Union soldiers and 18,000 Confederate soldiers
B) 33,000 Union soldiers and 15,000 Confederate soldiers
C) 42,000 Union soldiers and 28,000 Confederate soldiers
D) 45,000 Union soldiers and 16,000 Confederate soldiers

The correct answer is C:) 42,000 Union soldiers and 28,000 Confederate soldiers.

132) What was the blockade?

    A) The blockade was a line of Northerners that stood at the Southern ports to protect them.
    B) The blockade was a massive naval action that was set up on the Atlantic Ocean and Gulf coast.
    C) The blockade was a massive line of British ships that brought supplies to the Southern ports.
    D) The blockade was a hug line of British ships that safeguarded the Northern ships from blocking the Southern ports.

The correct answer is B:) The blockade was a massive naval action that was set up on the Atlantic Ocean and Gulf coast.

133) What were blockade runners?

    A) Ships that attempted to become apart of the blockade.
    B) British ships that carried cargo for the South.
    C) Ships that attempted to evade the blockade.
    D) British ships that attempted to help the North destroy the ports of the South.

The correct answer is C:) Ships that attempted to evade the blockade.

134) General Sherman was made famous for his?

    A) Strategies throughout the war
    B) March through the South
    C) Neckties
    D) His scorched earth policy

The correct answer C:) Neckties.

135) In a letter written by General Lee he stated he depended greatly on what?

    A) Blockade-runners to supply artillery
    B) Blockade ships to help with supplies
    C) Blockade-runners to supply shoes, blankets and leather for the winter
    D) Blockade-runners to supply food and water

The correct answer is C:) Blockade-runners to supply shoes, blankets and leather for the winter.

136) What was one of the main reasons for shortages?

  A) Poor distribution
  B) The conditions the railroads were in poor shape
  C) Bad management
  D) All of the above

The correct answer is D:) All of the above. All three reasons for the low supply of food in the South was poor distribution, the conditions the railroads were in poor shape and bad management.

137) What battles were fought during the Shenandoah Valley Campaign?

  A) Battle of Smithfield Crossing, Battle of Berryville, Battle of Opequon, Battle of Fisher's Hill, Battle of Tom's Brook and the Battle of Cedar Creek
  B) Battle of Guard Hill, the Battle of Summit point, Battle of Smithfield Crossing, Battle of Berryville, Battle of Opequon, Battle of Fisher's Hill, and Battle of Tom's Brook
  C) Battle of Guard Hill, the Battle of Summit point, Battle of Smithfield Crossing, Battle of Berryville, Battle of Opequon, Battle of Fisher's Hill, Battle of Tom's Brook and the Battle of Cedar Creek
  D) Battle of Summit point, Battle of Smithfield Crossing, Battle of Berryville, Battle of Opequon, and the Battle of Fisher's Hill

The correct answer is C:) Battle of Guard Hill, the Battle of Summit point, Battle of Smithfield Crossing, Battle of Berryville, Battle of Opequon, Battle of Fisher's Hill, Battle of Tom's Brook and the Battle of Cedar Creek.

138) What was the Navel's involvement in the Civil War?

  A) The Navy ran for materials for the Union from international countries.
  B) The Navy launched a series of amphibious assaults, called the blockade.
  C) The Navy offered the Union a series of Ironclad ships.
  D) The Navy offered the Union all their soldiers to help aid in the fighting against the Confederate forces.

The correct answer is B:) The Navy launched a series of amphibious assaults, called the blockade.

139) Lincoln's plans for reconstruction included?

    A) Lincoln's plan for reconstruction was to set up boundaries and camps within the South and the soldiers to fix the mess made by the war.

    B) Lincoln was motivated by a need to build a strong republican party in the South and end the bitterness between the North and the South. He issued a proclamation of amnesty and reconstruction in the area the Confederacy occupied by the Union Armies.

    C) Lincoln set up a plan to allow the South to continue with their state rights to decide for themselves whether or not they want slaves within their states and decide for themselves about reconstruction.

    D) Lincoln set up safety nets for freed blacks and vetoed all black codes, he offered.

The correct answer is B:) Lincoln was motivated by a need to build a strong republican party in the South and end the bitterness between the North and the South. He issued a proclamation of amnesty and reconstruction in the area the Confederacy occupied by the Union Armies.

140) Who was the Union General at Gettysburg?

    A) General Johnston
    B) General Meade
    C) General Grant
    D) General Sherman

The correct answer is B:) General Meade.

141) Where was Sherman planning on going to after he surrendered Atlanta and left with his army?

    A) Port Savannah
    B) The Potomac
    C) Cold Harbor
    D) Shenandoah Valley

The correct answer is A:) Port Savannah.

142) The assassination of Abraham Lincoln was when?

    A) April 16, 1865
    B) April 12, 1865
    C) April 14, 1865
    D) May 14, 1865

The correct answer is C:) April 14, 1865. April 14, 1865 was the date Lincoln was assassinated.

143) What was the original plan of Lincoln's assassinator?

    A) John Wilkes Booth hoped to cause the downfall of the Federal government by assassinating Lincoln, Seward and Johnson.
    B) John Wilkes Booth hoped to assassinate Lincoln and his entire cabinet.
    C) John Wilkes Booth hoped to cause the downfall of the Federal government by assassinating Lincoln.
    D) John Wilkes Booth wanted to assassinate Lincoln and his administration.

The correct answer is A:) John Wilkes Booth hoped to cause the downfall of the Federal Government by assassinating Lincoln, Seward and Andrew Johnson.

144) How did the plan of Lincoln's assassinator fail?

    A) Lincoln's administration counterattacked Booth leaving his entire plan destroyed, other then the assassination of Lincoln.
    B) The rest of the cabinet could not be found and only Lincoln was attacked that day.
    C) Lincoln and Seward was the only two Wilkes and his men could find, therefore were the only two who were assassinated.
    D) William Seward survived and the man he hired to assassinate Vice President Andrew Johnson failed to attack him.

The correct answer is D:) William Seward survived and the man he hired to assassinate Vice President Andrew Johnson failed to attack him. Booth had hoped to cause the downfall of the Federal Government by assassinating Lincoln, Seward and Andrew Johnson. Yet, William Seward survived and the man he hired to assassinate Vice President Andrew Johnson failed to attack him.

145) What was significant about the Battle of Vicksburg?

  A) It was the first Battle fought against Generals Grant and Lee.
  B) It gave control of the Mississippi River to the Union.
  C) It was the first significant battle of the Civil War.
  D) It was the first Union victory over the Confederate army.

The correct answer is B:) It gave control of the Mississippi River to the Union.

146) Upon the Fall of Richmond, what was Grant focused on preventing?

  A) Grant planned to attack the Confederates blind, while they were sleeping.
  B) Grant planned to cut off other Confederate troops from coming into Richmond.
  C) Grant planned to cut off the two railroads that continued to supply the Confederates and to extend his lines west around Richmond and Petersburg.
  D) Grant planned to bring Lee down by forcing him to surrender.

The correct answer is C:) Grant planned to cut off the two railroads that continued to supply the Confederates and to extend his lines west around Richmond and Petersburg.

147) Where was Jefferson Davis captured?

  A) Irwinville, Georgia
  B) Richmond
  C) Fort Monroe, Georgia
  D) Petersburg

The correct answer is A:) Irwinville, Georgia. Jefferson Davis was captured at Irwinville, Georgia on in May 1865.

148) What were the Black Codes?

  A) Laws that allowed citizen benefits to all freed black slaves.
  B) Laws that allowed freed blacks to vote, buy and sell property, and other political and economic rights.
  C) Laws that constricted civil rights and civil liberties of blacks, especially freed slaves.
  D) Laws that restricted Blacks from voting.

The correct answer is C:) Laws that constricted civil rights and civil liberties of blacks, especially freed slaves.

149) Upon the assassination of Lincoln, Vice President Johnson took over. His plan for reconstruction was?

A) He put into action the Black codes and pardoned Confederate leaders and allowed ex-Confederates to maintain control of the South, including governments, lands and blacks.
B) He planned to take over Lincoln's stance and plans on reconstruction.
C) He planned on making civil rights laws enacted into Congress, giving blacks the same rights as whites.
D) He planned on allowing Congress to decide and maintain a plan for reconstruction.

The correct answer is A:) He put into action the Black codes and pardoned Confederate leaders and allowed ex-Confederates to maintain control of the South, including governments, lands and blacks.

150) The response to Johnson's policy was?

A) It aroused intense opposition; they lashed out and denounced Republicans as traitors.
B) Congress and the South was satisfied with Johnson's policy.
C) Northerners were opposed to the Johnson's policy, but believed as the President he should have the knowledge to run the country.
D) Northerners lead rallies and demonstrations to impeach the President from power.

The correct answer is A:) It aroused intense opposition; they lashed out and denounced Republicans as traitors. Reconstruction aroused intense opposition, slaveholders and non-slaveholders in the South were bitter over the loss of the war, as slaveholders were upset over losing their slaves. They lashed out at the reconstruction and denounced Republicans as traitors to their race.

151) Johnston surrendered to General Sherman in 1865, what news did he learn of that made him surrender?

A) He learned of Lee's surrender
B) He learned that Union forces put an end to the Confederacy
C) He learned the war was over
D) He learned of Lincoln's assassination

The correct answer is A:) He learned of Lee's surrender. Johnston surrendered after he learned of Lee's Surrender.

152) The total cost of the war was?

    A) 2 million dollars
    B) More than half a million dollars
    C) 3.3 million
    D) 1.1 million

The correct answer B:) More than half a million dollars. The total cost of the war was more than a half million dollars, and after veterans care and compensation that number rose to 3.3 million.

153) How many lives in total were lost from the war?

    A) 850,000 lives were lost in the war
    B) 640,000 lives were lost in the war
    C) 1.1 million lives were lost during the war
    D) 2 million lives were lost during the war

The correct answer is C:) 1.1 Million lives were lost during the war.

154) What was the largest economic loss?

    A) More than 865,000 dollars of business and personal property was lost throughout the Civil War.
    B) More than a half billion dollars' worth of business and personal property was lost throughout the Civil War.
    C) More than 1 million dollars of farm stock was lost during the Civil War.
    D) More than 500,000 dollars of personal property was lost during the Civil War.

The correct answer is B:) More than a half billion dollars' worth of business and personal property was lost throughout the Civil War.

155) When did reconstruction begin?

    A) In the middle of the war
    B) At the end of the war
    C) At the beginning of the war
    D) After the assassination of Lincoln

The correct answer is A:) In the middle of the war.

156) Name the three eras of reconstruction.

    A) Presidential Reconstruction (1863), Radical Reconstruction (1866), and Redemption (1873)
    B) Presidential Reconstruction (1862-1868), Radical Reconstruction (1869-1872), and Redemption (1871-1875)
    C) The Presidential Reconstruction (1863-1866), Radical Reconstruction (1866-1873), and Redemption (1873-1877)
    D) The Presidential Reconstruction (1862-1867), Radical Reconstruction (1865-1876), and Redemption (1875-1879)

The correct answer is C:) The Presidential Reconstruction (1863-1866), Radical Reconstruction (1866-1873), and Redemption (1873-1877).

157) What led to the end of the Confederacy?

    A) The Fall of Richmond
    B) The surrender of Lee
    C) The surrender of Johnston
    D) Sherman's March through the South

The correct answer is A:) The Fall of Richmond.

158) Congressional reconstruction plans included?

    A) Congressional reconstruction planned to allow each state their own right to deal with reconstruction in their own way.
    B) Congressional reconstruction planned to put into action the civil rights and laws that concerned the rights of freed slaves.
    C) Congressional reconstruction adjourned in 1865 to leave the matters of reconstruction in the hands of President Lincoln.
    D) Congressional reconstruction wanted to ensure the Black codes were incorporated into the Constitution.

The correct answer is C:) Congressional reconstruction adjourned in 1865 to leave the matters of reconstruction in the hands of President Lincoln.

159) What was the plan of the Radical Republicans?

   A) They supported Presidential plans, but demanded that a more aggressive prosecution of the war should be pursued.
   B) They supported Federal civil rights but felt that the Presidential parties needed to ensure this.
   C) They supported Federal civil rights and allowed free slaves to vote in the South, all except ex-Confederates. They demanded that a more aggressive prosecution of the war and faster destruction of slavery should be implemented.
   D) They felt civil rights was wrong and demanded that a more aggressive prosecution of Northerners for attempting to demolish slavery should be implemented.

The correct answer is C:) They supported Federal civil rights and allowed free slaves to vote in the South, all except ex-Confederates. They demanded that a more aggressive prosecution of the war and faster destruction of slavery should be implemented.

160) What was the Fourteenth amendment?

   A) The fourteenth amendment requires that states provide protection under the law to all persons, granting all natural born or naturalized citizens federal and civil rights.
   B) The fourteenth amendment requires that states do not provide protection under the law to all persons, granting all natural born or naturalized citizens federal and civil rights.
   C) The fourteenth amendment requires that states provide protection under the law to only white persons.
   D) The fourteenth amendment requires that states provide protection under the law that only whites are natural born or naturalized citizens federal and civil rights.

The correct answer is A:) The fourteenth amendment requires that states provide protection under the law to all persons, granting all natural born or naturalized citizens federal and civil rights.

161) What was the fifteenth amendment?

    A) The fifteenth amendment states that the governments of the United States of America to prevent blacks from voting.

    B) The fifteenth amendment states that the governments of the United States of America may not prevent a person from voting, just because of his race, color, or previous condition of servitude.

    C) The fifteenth amendment states that the governments of the United States of America may prevent a person from voting, just because of his race, color, or previous condition of servitude.

    D) The fifteenth amendment states that the governments of the United States of America may not prevent a person from voting, just because of his race, color, but can prevent him for previous condition of servitude.

The correct answer is D:) The fifteenth amendment states that the governments of the United States of America may not prevent a person from voting, just because of his race, color, but can prevent him for previous condition of servitude.

162) What was the purpose if the Freedmen's Bureau?

    A) It was an agency to help freed slaves in the South, with shelter, housing and other essentials.

    B) It was an agency to help aid the Underground Railroad.

    C) It was an agency to help slaveholders to rebuild slavery after the Civil War.

    D) It was an agency to help freed slaves in the South to learn to read and write.

The correct answer is A:) It was an agency to help freed slaves in the South, with shelter, housing and other essentials.

163) The Civil Rights act was?

    A) The civil rights were acts that gave only voting rights to the freed slaves after the Civil War.

    B) The civil rights were acts that gave rights to the South slaveholders after the Civil War.

    C) The civil rights were acts that gave rights to the freed slaves after the Civil War.

    D) The civil rights were acts that gave rights to the freed slaves only the right to be free, without any rights of citizenship, after the Civil War.

The correct answer is C:) The civil rights were acts that gave rights to the freed slaves after the Civil War.

164) Before the Civil War, how many positions of power did blacks hold outside of the South?

    A) 137 black office holders lived outside the South
    B) 198 black office holders lived outside the South
    C) 147 black office holders lived outside the South
    D) 237 black office holders lived outside the South

The correct answer is A:) 137 black office holders lived outside the South.

165) The two most prominent scalawags were?

    A) Andrew Johnson and Joseph Brown
    B) General James Longstreet and Joseph Brown
    C) General James Longstreet and Edwin M. Stanton
    D) Edwin M. Stanton and Joseph Brown

The correct answer is B:) General James Longstreet and Joseph Brown.

166) What did Southerners consider to be redemption?

    A) An all white government
    B) The defeat of reconstruction by voting democrat
    C) A more accomplished reconstruction
    D) When all the scalawags came home

The correct answer is B:) The defeat of reconstruction by voting democrat. White majorities convinced most whites to vote democrat, this was enough to defeat the Reconstruction, which Southerners called redemption.

167) What was considered to be the end of Reconstruction?

    A) The end of reconstruction was complete once all Federal troops were withdrawn from the South.
    B) The end of reconstruction was when the war came to an end.
    C) The end of reconstruction was when all states were back in the Union.
    D) The end of reconstruction came when the North felt the South was ready to take over control of their states.

The correct answer is A:) The end of reconstruction was complete once all Federal troops were withdrawn from the South.

168) How was the Gettysburg Railroad Station used in the Gettysburg battle?

A) As a base of operations
B) As a hospital
C) As a kitchen
D) As a hiding place

The correct answer is B:) As a hospital.

169) A "bread riot" in which city became a sign of the desperate state of the South towards the end of the Civil War?

A) Richmond
B) New Orleans
C) Charleston
D) Augusta

The correct answer is A:) Richmond. Heavy inflation and blockades by the North had cut off the city of Richmond from necessary food and supplies. A group of women in Richmond decided to band together and demand food from the governor. The women rioted through the city.

170) Which of the following best describes a paper blockade?

A) A blockade that is maintained by small, poorly-armed ships
B) A blockade that targets primarily paper goods
C) A blockade that cannot be properly enforced
D) A blockade that is enforced primarily by written agreements between nations

The correct answer is C:) A blockade that cannot be properly enforced. This was the case when President Lincoln declared a blockade against the South early in the war, but was initially unable to enforce it.

171) After a pro-slavery group ransacked the city of Lawrence, abolitionist forces responded with the Pottawatomie Massacre led by

A) Daniel Webster
B) David Wilmot
C) John Brown
D) Jefferson Davis

The correct answer is C:) John Brown. Brown was a dedicated abolitionist who believed that the only way to end the conflict was to respond in kind. Under his direction five individuals were killed in the Pottawatomie Massacre.

172) Which element of the Compromise of 1850 was the most important to the South?

    A) No slavery restrictions in Utah
    B) Fugitive Slave Law
    C) Slaveholding permitted in Washington D.C.
    D) Slave trade prohibited in Washington D.C.

The correct answer is B:) Fugitive Slave Law. This law was a huge victory for the Southern states because it required the North to aid in the capture of escaped slaves. The victory was primarily symbolic, however, because there was very little effort made to enforce it in most Northern states.

173) In the Compromise of 1850

    A) Texas was admitted to the nation as a free state
    B) Utah was admitted to the nation as a free state
    C) Kentucky was admitted to the nation as a free state
    D) California was admitted to the nation as a free state

The correct answer is D:) California was admitted to the nation as a free state. This part of the compromise was favorable to the North because it left the balance of the Senate with the free states. However, California tended to follow the Southern states in terms of voting.

174) The majority of soldiers who participated in the Civil War were

    A) Volunteers in the North and conscripted in the South
    B) Volunteers in both the North and the South
    C) Conscripted in the North and volunteers in the South
    D) Conscripted in both the North and the South

The correct answer is B:) Volunteers in both the North and the South. Because of the personal importance that the war represented the majority of the soldiers in both armies were volunteers.

175) The Confederate States of America funded their war effort primarily by

A) Donations from citizens
B) Printing money
C) Trading with Mexico
D) Selling cotton

The correct answer is E:) Printing money. As a newly declared country the government of the CSA had the right to print their own currency, which they did in massive quantities. This led to devastating inflation before the war was over.

176) In Daniel Webster's famous "Seventh of March" speech, he

A) Announced his change of heart and desire to maintain the cause of emancipation
B) Encouraged all of the senators to vote against abolition
C) Spoke in favor of the Compromise of 1850 and stricter Fugitive Slave Laws
D) None of the above

The correct answer is C:) Spoke in favor of the Compromise of 1850 and stricter Fugitive Slave Laws. Particularly in his home state of Massachusetts, the public reaction to the speech was incredibly negative. People felt betrayed that Webster would seek so strongly against abolitionist causes. He soon resigned from Congress.

177) What were the primary weapons used in the Civil War?

A) Cannons
B) Bayonets
C) Minie Balls and Rifles
D) Swords

The correct answer is C:) Minie Balls and Rifles. The Civil War is often considered to be the first modern war because it is the first war in which weapons were available in mass produced quantities. The availability of minie balls, muskets, and rifles allowed the Civil War to be one of the most devastating in American history.

178) Rather than accept defeat, a number of Confederate soldiers escaped to

  A) California
  B) Canada
  C) Mexico
  D) Russia

The correct answer is C:) Mexico. Land was granted for several thousand men to settle in Mexico, but the privilege was revoked when the current leader fell from power. The men were forced to return to the United States.

179) Approximately how many soldiers died in the Civil War?

  A) 62,000
  B) 43,000
  C) 430,000
  D) 620,000

The correct answer is D:) 620,000. The Civil War was by far the most devastating conflict in the history of the United States. The combined casualties from all other wars totals to 644,000 – just recently surpassing the number of soldiers killed in the Civil War alone.

180) Which of the following states seceded latest in the War?

  A) Tennessee
  B) South Carolina
  C) Texas
  D) Virginia

The correct answer is A:) Tennessee. Tennessee was the last state to secede on June 8, 1861. The full order of secession was: South Carolina, Mississippi, Florida, Alabama, Georgia, Louisiana, Texas, Virginia, Arkansas, North Carolina, Tennessee.

181) Which were the first seven states to secede from the Union?

    A) North Carolina, Alabama, Florida, Georgia, Virginia, Mississippi, and Arkansas

    B) South Carolina, Mississippi, Alabama, Georgia, Texas, Virginia, and North Carolina

    C) South Carolina, Mississippi, Florida, Alabama, Georgia, Louisiana, and Texas

    D) Tennessee, North Carolina, Arkansas, Virginia, Texas, Louisiana, and Georgia

The correct answer is C:) South Carolina, Mississippi, Florida, Alabama, Georgia, Louisiana, and Texas. The secessions came in two waves, these first seven seceding early in 1861, with Tennessee, North Carolina, Arkansas, and Virginia following several months later.

182) States which were in support of slavery and other Southern political ideas but did not secede from the Union were known as

    A) Southern states

    B) Non-Confederate states

    C) Unionist states

    D) Border states

The correct answer is D:) Border states. Despite many efforts to remain neutral, these states were heavily involved in conflicts because of their central locations.

183) One of the major concerns solved by the Missouri Compromise was

    A) The need to maintain a balance of slave states and free states

    B) The legality of the threats of secession being made by many states

    C) Worry that Indians would lose additional rights if slavery were allowed

    D) The desire for more Northern states to support slavery

The correct answer is A:) The need to maintain a balance of slave states and free states. The compromise allowed for Missouri to be admitted as a slave state, and Maine as a free state. This allowed for the balance of slave states and free states to remain constant.

184) The Wilmot Proviso stated that

    A) The balance between slave states and free states must be maintained
    B) Slavery would never be allowed in any territories won from Mexico
    C) California could be admitted as a state only if the North were free and the South allowed slavery
    D) The balance of the Senate must not be either pro slavery or abolitionist

The correct answer is B:) Slavery would never be allowed in any territories won from Mexico. Despite several attempts by the House of Representatives to pass this Proviso into effect, it never received the needed majority in the evenly split Senate.

185) Which Constitution specifically grants the right of secession to a state?

    A) Constitution of the United States of America
    B) Constitution of the Confederate States of America
    C) Both
    D) Neither

The correct answer is D:) Neither. The Constitution of the Confederate States made several alterations to the original - including provisions ensuring the continued legality of slave ownership. However, neither Constitution specifically mentions the right of a state to secede.

186) After the Civil War, the South's representation in the House of Representatives

    A) Increased
    B) Decreased
    C) Remained constant
    D) Cannot be determined

The correct answer is A:) Increased. Prior to the war the slave populations in Southern states were given a three-fifths count towards their population to determine representation. After the war those individuals were counted normally with the rest of the population. This resulted in the South receiving greater representation in the House of Representatives.

187) The strategic high-ground position of Marye's Heights was instrumental in Confederate victory at which location?

A) Fredericksburg
B) Antietam
C) Gettysburg
D) Fort Sumter

The correct answer is A:) Fredericksburg. This was among the greatest of Confederate victories in the war. Despite being outnumbered, Union deaths were more than double that of Confederate deaths. This was a great boost of morale to the Confederate soldiers.

Test Taking Strategies

Here are some test-taking strategies that are specific to this test and to other DSST tests in general:

- Keep your eyes on the time. Pay attention to how much time you have left.
- Read the entire question and read all the answers. Many questions are not as hard to answer as they may seem. Sometimes, a difficult sounding question really only is asking you how to read an accompanying chart. Chart and graph questions are on most DANTES/DSST tests and should be an easy free point.
- If you don't know the answer immediately, the new computer-based testing lets you mark questions and come back to them later if you have time .
- Read the wording carefully. Some words can give you hints to the right answer. There are no exceptions to an answer when there are words in the question such as always, all or none. If one of the answer choices includes most or some of the right answers, but not all, then that is not the answer. Here is an example:

    The primary colors include all of the following:

    A) Red, Yellow, Blue, Green
    B) Red, Green, Yellow
    C) Red, Orange, Yellow
    D) Red, Yellow, Blue

    Although item A includes all the right answers, it also includes an incorrect answer, making it incorrect. If you didn't read it carefully, were in a hurry, or didn't know the material well, you might fall for this.
- Make a guess on a question that you do not know the answer to. There is no penalty for an incorrect answer. Eliminate the answer choices that you know are incorrect. For example, this will let your guess be a 1 in 3 ch ance instead.

Test Preparation

How much you need to study depends on your knowledge of a subject area. If you are interested in literature, took it in school, or enjoy reading then your study and preparation for the literature or humanities test will not need to be as intensive as that of someone who is new to literature.

This book is much different than the regular DANTES study guides. This book actually teaches you the information that you need to know to pass the test. If you are particularly interested in an area, or feel that you want more information, do a quick search online. We've tried not to include too much depth in areas that are not as essential on the test. Everything in this book will be on the test. It is important to understand all major theories and concepts listed in the table of contents. It is also important to know any bolded words.

Don't worry if you do not understand or know a lot about the area. With minimal study, you can complete and pass the test.

To prepare for the test, make a series of goals. Determine a certain amount of time to review the information you have already studied and to learn additional material. Take notes as you study; it will help you learn the material.

Legal Note

FLASHCARDS

This section contains flashcards for you to use to further your understanding of the material and test yourself on important concepts, names or dates. Read the term or question then flip the page over to check the answer on the back. Keep in mind that this information may not be covered in the text of the study guide. Take your time to study the flashcards, you will need to know and understand these concepts to pass the test.

15th Amendment	Freedmen's Bureau
14th Amendment	The Battle of the Wilderness was how many days?
What was America's bloodiest campaign?	Emancipation Proclamation
Bloodiest one-day battle in history	Who was made famous for the saying "All quiet on the Potomac"?

It was an agency to help freed slaves in the South, with shelter, housing and other essentials

The governments may not prevent a person from voting, just because of this race, color, or previous condition of servitude

Two days

States provide protection under the law to all persons, granting all natural born or naturalized citizens federal and civil rights

An order that declared the freedom of all slaves

Cold Harbor

McClellan

Antietam

Bull Run is also known as what name?

Who invented the cotton gin?

Did the Know Nothing Party encourage or discourage immigration?

Who was Dred Scott?

What did the Supreme Court rule regarding slavery in the Dred Scott Decision?

Who said "I, _____, am now quite certain that the crimes of this guilty land will never be purged away but with blood"?

Who had the nickname "stonewall"?

What was the end of the reconstruction?

Eli Whitney

First Manassas

A slave who sued for freedom

Discourage

John Brown

That slaves were property and had no rights

The end of reconstruction was complete once all federal troops were withdrawn from the South

General Thomas Jackson

Carpetbagger

Who were the two most prominent scalawags?

The three areas of reconstruction

What was the main Southern crop?

What was the 2nd main Southern crop?

House slaves were what?

The Black codes

Where was Jefferson Davis captured?

General James Longstreet
and Joseph Brown

Someone who was against
slavery that moved to the
South after the war

Cotton

Presidential reconstruction,
radical reconstruction, and
redemption

Slaves that worked in the
plantation main houses

Rice

Irwinville, Georgia

Laws that constricted civil
rights and civil liberties of
blacks, especially freed
slaves

What day was Abraham Lincoln assassinated?

Who assassinated Lincoln?

What are Sherman's neck-ties?

What is the Ku Klux Klan?

Who was a founding father of the Ku Klux Klan?

The Savanna Campaign was also known as

How many casualties were there at Gettysburg?

Copperheads

John Wilkes Booth

April 14, 1865

An anti-black group

Railroad ties bent around trees

Sherman's March to the Sea

General Forest

Peace Democrats from the North who opposed the Civil War and Lincoln and his administration

51,000

The first official black infantry

Women volunteered as what in the war?

What was the leading cause of death the in war?

President of the Confederate States of America

Which was the first state to secede from the Union?

Which state united the South for slavery?

Senator Stephen A. Douglas

What was the Compromise of 1850?

Nurses

The 54th Massachusetts
Volunteer Infantry

Jefferson Davis

Disease

South Carolina

South Carolina

Admit California as a free
state and let future states
decide for themselves the
issue of slavery

Initiated the Kansas-
Nebraska Act

Who wrote *Uncle Tom's Cabin*?

Who wrote *American Slavery as It Is: Testimony of a Thousand Witnesses*?

Abolition movement means what?

1st Amendment

What country did most of the immigrants come from in the early 1800s?

What year was *Uncle Tom's Cabin* published?

Who could send a substitute?

What was the underground railroad?

Theodore Dwight Weld

Harriett Beecher Stowe

Congress shall make
no law respecting an
establishment of religion,
or prohibiting the free
exercise thereof

People against slavery

1852

Ireland

A way for slaves to escape
to the North

Anyone who could pay the
cost for someone else to
serve in the war for them